The Angels of Alchemy

Contact the 42 Angels of Magickal Transformation

Damon Brand

Copyright © 2016 Damon Brand

All Rights Reserved. This book may not be reproduced, in whole or in part, in any form or by any means electronic or mechanical, including photocopying, recording, or by any information storage retrieval system now known or hereafter invented, without written permission from the publisher, The Gallery of Magick.

Disclaimer: Consider all information in this book to be speculation and not professional advice, to be used at your own risk. Damon Brand and The Gallery of Magick are not responsible for the consequences of your actions. Success depends on the integrity of your workings, the initial conditions of your life and your natural abilities, so results will vary. The information is never intended to replace or substitute for medical advice from a professional practitioner, and when it comes to issues of physical health, mental health or emotional conditions, no advice is given or implied, and you should always seek conventional, professional advice. The information is provided on the understanding that you will use it in accordance with the laws of your country.

I would like to express my sincere thanks to Zanna Blaise, whose contributions to this text are considerable. Without her groundwork, perceptions and clarifications, this book would not have been possible.

Damon Brand

CONTENTS

The Process of Alchemy	9
Preparing Your Ritual	15
Tasking the Angels	19
The Essence of Results	27
Working the Magick	33
The 42 Angels of Transformation	37
Pronunciation Guide	123
The Evocation of Angels	127
The Experience of Evocation	131
The Affinity Process	139
The Evocation Keys	153
The Hidden Power of Evocation	161
The Source of Angelic Knowledge	163
Working with Magick	169

The Process of Alchemy

Alchemy is a process of change. The angels revealed in this book enable you to access personal alchemy, to change who you are, to refine yourself at the deepest level and thus attract the life you desire.

The angels can help you to find patience, endurance and persistence, so that you can complete projects to your satisfaction. There are angels that can speed up the flow of reality, to help bring about rapid change, and angels that work to purify and clarify your emotions. They provide emotional balance and sustenance, while giving insight into situations, revealing the easiest way to get where you want to be.

The angels can aid your spiritual development and clarify the desires that lie within. These angels can support your ability to maintain integrity when faced with compromise, and give you the power to project charisma. By working with the angels you can develop your imaginative abilities and intuition. The angels can restore confidence, inspire your thoughts and help you to see visions, to obtain mystical guidance.

This is a subtle and sophisticated magick, that gets the results you want by an indirect route. Rather than tackling the obvious symptoms of a problem, it works on aspects of your inner being to reorder your life. By undergoing personal transformation, you can obtain the life you want.

If you want a better relationship, cultivate the best in yourself to improve that relationship. If you want to attract more joy, you make changes to your ability to receive joy. When you seek happiness, you purify elements of yourself that block your progress to pleasure. Although subtle in its approach, the results obtained via this magickal pathway can be profound.

This book contains two methods for working with the forty-two angels. In the first method, you charge the angel to complete a task in accordance with that angel's primary power. In essence, you ask for the angel to bring about the change in yourself. This first method is known as tasking.

In the second method, you call the angel into your presence, so that you can sense it directly. The more skilled will be able to see the angels, and converse with them. This second method is known as evocation. The purpose of such evocation is to receive wisdom, guidance and change more directly.

The powers conveyed by these angels are immense, because they help to refine you, connecting you to your deepest self, making it easier to progress through life, attracting the situations and people that will bring you the most happiness. When things are difficult, these angels offer sanctuary and emotional healing.

If you seek change, these angels can guide and encourage change. While a large proportion of the magick that we have shared with the world is about obtaining results by influencing the people and situations that surround you, the focus of this magick is on yourself. When you have a need, the angels can encourage change within you, and that change attracts the future you desire.

We refer to these spirits as The Angels of Alchemy, because they help to inspire change. Alchemy has many definitions, but is often seen as an act of transmutation, most notably the transformation of base metals into gold. In the context of this book, alchemy is symbolic of the transformation that occurs within the self.

The angelic alchemy in this book is a process of connecting to your own development, and embracing the changes that can bring you the most fulfilling life. This magick recognizes that a great deal of spiritual development can be obtained by embracing physical pleasures, and the joys of interacting with the material world. It focuses on your connection to your inner self, and the emotions that can sometimes guide, sometimes conceal, what it is you truly want. By working this magick you will come to know yourself, and with that knowledge, cultivate yourself, and bring about the life you desire.

It should be said from the outset that direct evocation is not simple, which is why the initial focus of this book is on tasking the angels through a more straightforward method. Using a simple ritual, you connect with the angel, and obtain the result you seek. For most people, tasking works easily, and will be all the magick you need. If you want to take things to a more advanced level, you have the option of evocation, calling the angel to appear before you. The evocation process, although more straightforward than many of the ultra-complex rituals of tradition, remains challenging. It is considered worthwhile by the ambitious, because it does enable direct communication and interaction to take place.

The Gallery of Magick aims to simplify magickal practice, leaving only what is essential for success, but evocation is a form of magick that requires skill and persistence to obtain results. You are, after all, attempting to bring an angel into your immediate experience, so this cannot be achieved with wishful thinking or a quick wave of a wand.

In fact, you won't need a wand, or any other tools. All you need is your genuine desire, and the willingness to work the instructions with dedication. There is no need to create salt circles, light candles, burn incense or burden yourself with the paraphernalia of magick. For those who like such aspects of magick, they remain optional, but they are absolutely not required for success. It's far more valuable to work on your own pathway into magick, than on the devices of ritual.

If you only want to see results, I recommend that you start with the task-based approach to angel magick, so that you can request change, and see the results manifest in your life. Evocation is for the patient and dedicated, to be approached when you feel a desire for deeper communion with the angels.

There is no reason that evocation cannot be achieved by

a complete newcomer to magick. Indeed, as a newcomer you may be less burdened by dogma and tradition, and achieve astonishing results on your first attempt. But whatever your level of experience, do not let evocation be your only focus. Do not evoke out of a need for proof of angelic reality. If you want proof, performing magick consistently and seeing results is all you need. Proof should only ever come as a side-effect of your magickal practice. It should be the change itself that you seek, rather than the shock, drama and supernatural thrill of contact with an angel. You are undertaking this magickal work to make progress in your life. You are not a thrill-seeker looking to experience angelic contact purely for the delight of the experience.

Although this book is self-contained, it can be used to support your other magickal efforts. I have been saying for some time that indirect magick is one of the best ways to get what you really want, which is why I generally advise readers to look for *The 72 Sigils of Power* by Zanna Blaise, which, like this volume, focuses mostly on changes to the self. Self-change is often the key to obtaining external results. If you're using money magick, and not getting results, it's not because you need better, stronger money magick. It's because you need to make changes to your ability to receive money.

I strongly recommend that if you are working any other form of magick, that you use the rituals in this book, along with *The 72 Sigils of Power*, to refine yourself, making manifestation more likely. With that said, you do not need to buy anything else, or study any other magick, if you want to get started and see results. Everything you need to undergo personal transformation through the magick of alchemy can be found within these pages.

The book is set out as follows. In the opening chapters I show how you can work with the angels to have your needs met, via personal transformation. The book then presents the names, sigils and calls of the forty-two angels. Following this I explore the Affinity Process of Evocation, along with The Keys of Evocation for each angel. The book also contains a pronunciation guide, and closes with some background information about the angels and divine names, and a few additional ideas that can help the magick to work. The primary focus of the book is on practical magick that achieves results through inner change.

Preparing Your Ritual

In each chapter you will see a description of the angel's powers, and you should take the time to read through these, gaining an intuition about how each angel could help you. Although the descriptions are sometimes brief, this is deliberate, as your attempt to understand an angel, based on its name and concise description, causes you to mentally, spiritually and psychically *reach for the angel*. You begin to wonder about the angel. This act of reaching out with your curiosity is an important part of making contact with the angels. So read the descriptions, observe the sigils, and see if you can gain an insight into how an angel could be helpful.

Following the description of each angel, you will see a set of eight divine names and words of power, followed by the angel's name, all written phonetically. That means you say everything as though it is written in English. This is very easy, but it's worth reading the Pronunciation Guide at the end of the book to make sure you can feel at ease with the pronunciations.

Before the ritual begins, get used to saying these words. Know that the final word in the list is the phonetic pronunciation of the angel's name. So for the angel Orpaniel, it is OAR-PAH-KNEE-ELL. You will repeat this many times, later in the ritual.

Following this list of words there is an angelic sigil that looks something like this:

Using Hebrew letters, the divine names and words of power appear in the outer ring, and the angel's name is written in large letters in the center of the circle.

The ritual can be performed once on any given day, but you should decide in advance on how many days you will work the ritual. In many traditions, you are advised to perform a ritual a set number of times. In *The 72 Angels of Magick*, for example, you call on the angels for eleven successive days (starting on a Thursday). In *Words of Power*, however, you perform the ritual just once. In this book, you should be guided by your intuition. Be wary of being guided by fear, desperation or an eagerness to do more magick to force a result. Before you begin the ritual, make a decision to perform the ritual for a set number of days. These days may be consecutive, or you may choose to perform the ritual once a week, for two months, for example. Or it might be every other day for a week. Sometimes, you'll know that performing the ritual just once is enough. Trust your intuition.

You should then adhere to this decision, even if the result shows up early, or even if you feel that the magick should go on for longer. By establishing a set number of days, you ensure that you commit to those days fully.

Many people find this a challenge, and spend a great deal of time worrying about how many days they should perform the ritual for. Two, three, fifty? If you feel that your intuition is absolutely lacking, then perform the ritual for seven consecutive days. Otherwise, choose a number that feels right, and use that. You can perform the ritual at any time of the day or night.

Once the ritual has been completed, you may wonder if it needs to be repeated. Often, people wait for a result, and worry that they need to apply more magick to get that result. The trick here is to stop waiting altogether. As you will see, the magickal process involves an *expectation* of the change you desire, so waiting is more like hoping or wishing. Hoping and wishing are aspects of fear and doubt, so are best avoided. Assume that the magick will work.

If circumstances change, you can of course repeat the ritual. So, let's say that you perform a ritual to improve your confidence, and it works, gradually increasing your confidence over the coming weeks. There's no need to repeat anything. But if, months later, you find that you need even more confidence to rise to a new level of ease in your work relationships, for example, you could repeat the ritual. Any time that circumstances change, you can repeat, but be wary of just doing the ritual again in the hope that you will force the magick to work faster. This magick works on very subtle aspects of yourself, so rushing and pushing won't make it happen any faster. If you want faster results, cultivate patience.

Tasking the Angels

In this chapter I set out the entire procedure for tasking an angel. This means that you contact the angel using a ritual, and then set a task for that angel to complete. This is not a task in the sense of fetching riches or fortune, but the task of guiding you to personal transformation.

If you have read *The Angels of Love*, by Zanna Blaise, you will see that this is the same process, with a few minor variations. Here it can be applied to all forty-two angels, rather than the six that appeared in her book.

Find a time and place where you can obtain some peace and privacy. If you are ever interrupted in the middle of a ritual, you can simply stop, and no harm will be done, but the magick will not work until completed. It is wise to plan carefully, and find the time and space to perform magick without disturbance. Silence is not essential, but you should not be glancing at social media, watching TV or engaging in distractions while performing magick. Focus on what you are doing. Some people like to light a candle or put on calm or inspiring music, but for most people, you need nothing more than to take a few deep breaths, and know that you are entering a calm space where you can perform magick.

When you have chosen the appropriate angel, scan your eyes over the letters in the outer circle, starting at the top and moving your gaze anti-clockwise around the circle. This means that when you reach the bottom of the circle, your eyes will pass over letters that are upside down, and this is perfectly ok. During this letter scan you are not trying to read the words (even if you *can* read Hebrew), but nor are you staring. You are simply observing the letter shapes, and letting them ease into your inner mind. This is a simple process that only requires you to observe the letter shapes, calmly, passively, as you circle your eyes anti-clockwise, three times.

You now speak the divine words that accompany the specific angels. So for Orpaniel, those words would be:

> ZAHD-KEY-ELL
> UB-AH-GEE-TAHTZ
> AH-DEER-EAR-AWE-TZ
> BAH-HEAR-EAR-AWE-TZ
> GUH-VEER-YAH-RAWN
> YEEG-BAH-YAH

TUH-LAHM-YAH
TZ-TAHN-YAH

OAR-PAH-KNEE-ELL

You will notice that the final word is the Angel's name. You now scan your eyes over the angel's name, while repeating that angel name out loud, over and over again. Move your eyes from right to left, and simply take in the shape of the letters, without trying to read. You do not have to time the spoken words to match the visual scan. It's as easy as moving your gaze over the letters, slowly enough to see their shape, while repeating the angel's name.

The process of scanning over the letter shapes, while saying the angel's name, leads to you forming a connection with the angel. You should speak the angel's name out loud, even if it's a whisper. If you have no choice but to work in silence, *imagine* speaking the name loudly. You are talking *to* the angel, rather than saying the name without purpose. Think of this as a call to the angel, to make the angel aware of you, rather than as a repetitive chant. Even though you repeat the name, you do so to make contact. You are calling a name rather than chanting a magick word.

This form of magick is not evocation, so the contact you experience will be mild. The idea is to get the angel to know your request, and that is all you need, so if you feel little or no contact, you can still get results. If, after a few moments, you sense the angelic presence, you can stop saying the name, because contact has been established. You may sense a slight change in temperature, or feel a slight breeze, detect a scent, feel a change in the atmosphere or simply *know* that the angel is with you.

Sometimes, you will feel absolutely nothing at all. Some people never feel anything at this stage, and it is very important for me to reassure you that this is absolutely ok. You can perform rituals without sensing the presence of the angels, and your request will still be heard. Although you perform this part of the ritual with the aim of establishing contact, the sensation of contact is not the purpose.

Imagine you call a friend, and your friend answers the phone, but does not speak; it takes some trust for you to speak to the silence on the other end of the line. But you can speak, and you will be heard. That is what you do here. You know that the lines of communication have been opened.

As I say above, if you sense a connection, trust it, and move to the next step. If you feel nothing, simply continue with the repetition for about two minutes. At this point, you need to accept that contact has been made. Trust that this is the case, even if you feel nothing, and proceed *as though* the contact is very clear and real. If you doubt the connection, or worry that you've not done a good enough job, you undermine your magick. Instead, be confident, and know that this process of working with the sigil and saying the angel's name *will* establish contact.

You now make your request. Keep your eyes on the sigil, because it is a gateway that connects you to the angel. Your gaze can be loose, and you can blink, but you keep the sigil gently in view. Direct your words, feelings and thoughts to the sigil, because through your magickal work it has become a doorway to the consciousness of the angel. The method works whether the sigil is being used in an eBook, or a paperback, or even a copy you've made for your personal use, because it is the image of the sigil that makes the connection, rather than its physical presence.

Speak the angel's name, because you are addressing the angel, and then continue with your request. Speak your request, plainly, honestly and from the heart, without sounding defensive or apologetic for the request you make. Imagine that you are contacting Iophiel, the Angel of Beauty. Having read about the angel's powers you might phrase your request as something like this: 'Iophiel, I ask that you help me to infuse my creative writing with great beauty.' It can be that simple. You do not need to explain why, or justify your request. There is no need to elaborate, so long as you are clear about what you want. When you have a clear desire that can be summarised briefly, you will get results.

Be wary of adding in too much detail. Sometimes, requests go like this: 'Iophiel, I ask that you help to give my new novel more beauty, and help me find a way to make the main character more interesting, as well as making the plot more appealing. If you could make my words sound more beautiful, so that the prose is easier on the ear, that would be good.' This sort of communication *is* possible when you evoke an angel, but at this stage and with this style of task-based magick, *do not* make your request so complex. Summarise your needs into a simple, attainable result that can be defined and communicated with one or two sentences. It may help to plan what you will say in advance, or you may prefer to speak from the heart in the moment of ritual. This is a matter of personal choice, but you may find that the results are more potent if you allow the request to come out clearly in a moment of inspired truth.

As you speak you will feel the sincerity of your request. This is an important aspect of the ritual, and one that perhaps requires little guidance. You are asking for a change that you genuinely desire, so the sincerity should be in your words. But I think it is worth saying that you should ask with feeling. Do not sound desperate, do not beg or plead, but when you ask, put some emotion in your voice, to convey how you feel. Allow yourself to feel this desire. If you want more beauty in your creative work, this is not just a minor whim. It is something you genuinely require. You're not ordering pizza, so feel the request, rather than just speaking it. You do not need to drum up a deeply potent emotion that brings tears to your eyes. Just feel what you feel, rather than saying the words as a flat, empty request.

To conclude the ritual, you give thanks, and allow yourself to feel that you are thanking the angel because the magick *has already worked*. Imagine that you have been granted the result you ask. Imagine days or weeks have passed, and you are looking back with gratitude, feeling grateful that your dream has been realised. In the example given hear, you imagine that your creative work is now much more beautiful and inspired, and you notice how grateful you feel, and at this point you say *thank you* to the angel.

To do this, you think the angel's name in your mind, while looking at the sigil, and then say a brief *thank you* out loud while still gazing at the sigil, and maintaining the feeling of gratitude for the wish fulfilled.

(Ideally, you should *think* the angel's name, while saying *thank you* out loud. If you absolutely have to work in silence, think the angel's name, and then think *thank you* – all the while maintaining that emotion of gratitude for the result having already happened.)

Bear in mind that you are not thanking the angel simply for existing, or for listening to your request. You are thanking the angel for the magick, for having made the change that you request. Yes, this seems strange, because you are thanking before the result has actually happened. By doing this you are playing with time, and nudging reality. You act as though the magick has happened, and your gratitude seals the reality of that change.

Remember that you are not hoping for a result, or looking forward to what you will get. You capture the feeling of looking back, as though time has passed, and you now have exactly what you want. This feeling of achievement, of having got what you asked for, creates the emotion of gratitude. It may take a little practice, but becomes very easy with time.

Zanna Blaise put it best when she said, 'Pretending it's real *now*, you make it a thousand times more likely to be real in your future life. This is a way of clarifying to the angel how you want to feel. Once the angel knows how you want to feel, it will change reality to make you feel that way.'

The angels have a sacred duty to respond to requests that come from the heart, so remember that your *thank you* is polite and respectful, but you are not begging or worshiping the angel. You speak with respect and sincerity, and that is enough.

Everything I've described here takes only a few minutes. Saying the opening words, calling on the angel and establishing contact, speaking your request, and then capturing a moment of gratitude, can take less than a couple of minutes. In some cases, it takes longer, but you do not need to stretch this out to make it feel more potent. A ritual performed with deep focus and pinpoint concentration on your emotions, will be more powerful than one that drags on for no good reason.

That is the essence of the ritual, but there is more that you need to know. In the next chapter I look at how you can encourage the result to manifest.

The Essence of Results

The magick in this book is largely aimed at yourself. You will find that the listed powers talk about your feelings, your perception and your own sense of pleasure. There are a few exceptions. Gavoriel, for example, can help restore a sense of peace to a household. You should know, however, that the angel still works this magick through *you*. Gavoriel helps you to emanate love and peace, so that others sense it. The magick focuses on your personal relationship to reality.

Magick involves a subtle interplay of action and passivity. To obtain results it is essential that you contribute your own effort to obtaining the results, but it is also vital that you surrender the urgent need for a result. Although this may sound difficult and frustrating, it is easier than you might first think, and is a skill that improves with practice.

The good news is that when working on personal transformation, this is less of a problem. When you're doing conventional magick to make money, find love or obtain something concrete in the real world, it is very tempting to monitor the magick, to keep checking to see if it's worked. Letting go of the lust for result can be quite a challenge. But with the personal magick explored in this book, the results ease their way into your life, and you will find that lust for result is less of a problem. Despite this, you should still be aware that being too eager and impatient for the magick to work will often make the magick slower to manifest. It's not that the angels see your eagerness and withhold the result; it's that you are not open to receiving change. Understanding and experiencing this can be one of the greatest moments of magick.

A good way to go about things is to perform the magick, accept that it will work, but then go about making changes as though the magick never happened. That's your contribution, and it inspires the angels to respond. With money magick, for example, I often say that if you want to improve your sales, you should do magick to help with finances, and perform magick that works on your sales, but once the rituals have been performed you don't sit there waiting for better sales. You do everything you can to improve your sales, from working on your advertising and presentation, to learning new selling skills. People often think, 'But the whole point of magick is that it's a shortcut, a quicker, easier way to get where I want to be.' This is certainly true, but the great thing is that the smallest contribution of effort from you is magnified over and over by magick. If you do nothing, there's nothing to magnify. If you make changes, then magick can work to make those changes flow more effectively into your life. A small contribution of effort from you is the key that unlocks results.

If you read contributions to The Gallery of Magick website, you will hear many stories of rituals that were forgotten and then manifested in unexpected ways, without any observable effort on the part of the person who worked the ritual. These stories are wonderful, and I have experienced many such situations myself, but I believe that to get more consistent results you should approach magick as a collaboration. You are handing over one aspect of the work to the angels. This is the mystical, supernatural aspect, where chance and synchronicity play a part. Rather than hoping and wishing and trying to change your life with pure willpower, you ask the angels to do their part, by working with these supernatural aspects of reality. At the same time, you collaborate with the process by being engaged with the problem or challenge in the real world.

Imagine that you are shifting furniture in your house. You ask a friend to help you move the table, and then as your friend helps take the weight, you let go of the table, sit down and expect your friend to move the table. It's going to stay right where it is. But if you do your part, and lift gently, you'll get that table exactly where you want it to be in just a few seconds, without much effort. It's easier, because you asked for help, and it happens because you contribute. Also, you calmly expect that your friend will help, without doubt and fear. You know that your request is reasonable, and that your friend wants to help, so the help comes. This is how magick works. You make a request, politely and respectfully, without begging, and you expect the help, and you do your part. It doesn't need to be too complicated.

I have often heard a rather cynical response to this, along the lines of, 'But if I'm putting in all that extra effort, I may as well not bother with magick.' The way I see it is that by doing your part and making your contribution, you are enacting your decision. You are enacting your desire for change. By taking action you are attempting to change reality, and when that action is combined with magick, reality gives way to your desires far more readily than would otherwise be possible.

In terms of the personal transformation explored in this book, what contributions can you make? Say you've called Tzadkiel to give you an improved sense of authority at work, is there anything you can actually do? There are several things you might do, from the mundane and practical to the meditative and contemplative. You may read widely on the subject of personal authority, or you may simply attempt to stay aware of moments when you can exercise an air of authority. Perhaps you will spend some time each day meditating on your personal sense of authority. These ideas, and many others, can all work. Whatever you contribute, it will make a difference, so long as it is a sincere attempt to make change. I should remind you that the magick will work in ways you can't imagine, often beyond your expectation, but it will do so most effectively when you do *something* to actively enable the magick. So here, you would contribute to the result by working on your innate sense of authority.

When you are seeking personal change, actively working toward that change can be a challenge. If you're working magick for improved confidence, how can you actively try to be more confident? You can't just fake it. No, you can't, but you can do *something*. For some, the contribution would involve study and research about confidence, and putting into practice what you have learned. For others, it would be about testing personal limits; if you feel nervous at parties, you might make sure you go to a few, to push the limits of your confidence. And for others, it might be about simply allowing the feeling of confidence to arise as you repeat the ritual. All these approaches are valid. So long as you don't just do the ritual, sit back and hope for a result, something will happen.

The effort you make does not need to be detailed, extreme or particularly taxing. You are, after all, asking the magick to make a supernatural change, so the magick will do most of the work. So long as you do some. Make sure you do something, however small, to open yourself up to the required change.

If you call on Shemshiel to illuminate the blockages in your life, how could you contribute to that magick? You might stay open to signs and omens. You might make time to reflect, or sit quietly, allowing thoughts to arise around these blockages. Or you might spend time talking to a close friend about where you are in life, and notice the nudges of intuition that occur when you have the conversation. Any of these approaches can help, and all are better than sitting back and waiting for illumination.

If you're working with Nachliel, to relieve feelings of pain and overwhelm, how could you possibly contribute to that result? If you trust your intuition, once the ritual is underway, you may find that you give yourself more time to reflect, enjoy or explore other areas of your life. Or you may sit quietly, and observe your feelings, letting them release. Your contribution can be subtle and without strain.

It would be possible to write several more chapters on this subject, giving countless examples, but from what I have seen when using this magick, and when teaching it to others, you should be guided by your intuition. You will get a sense of what you can do to contribute to the magick. Trust your instincts, and make whatever small change you can. It might be nothing more than spending some time thinking about, or meditating upon, the result you are trying to achieve. Do that each day, and you are contributing to the magick.

Your contribution to the magick should start on the day that you begin the ritual, when possible, and should continue in the days after the ritual. There are no set rules about how much of a contribution you should make, because it's more about tuning into the result you want. You shouldn't get to bedtime and think, 'Oh no, I forgot to make my contribution to the magick.' Instead, your move toward the change should seep into your life, so that your contribution is an inevitable part of the day.

If you find this aspect of the magick baffling, and cannot think of a way to contribute to the magick, then modify the ritual slightly. When you have made your request, but before you say *thank you*, sit in contemplation. You remain in the presence of the angel, keeping your focus only on the angel's presence, allowing whatever thoughts occur to occur, but always coming back to your sense of the angel's presence. (If you can't actually feel the presence, that is ok. You only need to mentally acknowledge that the angel *is* there. Repeating the angel's name can help to re-establish the contact if it fades, or if you feel distracted.) There is nothing more to it than that. You sit for a while, letting the magick work if it will, and not caring if nothing happens yet, because you know it will eventually. Some people like to add a few minutes of contemplation to the ritual in this way, even if they plan to make other contributions to the magick. This is a personal choice, and does not need to be consistent, so allow yourself to sit in contemplation when it appeals.

Working the Magick

To ensure that the process of angelic tasking is made clear, I will give three specific examples to illustrate how you might perform a ritual. As the basic ritual structure is identical for each, you will note some repetition. Please note that this is intentional, and should actually assist you with becoming familiar with the ritual process. This can be an effective way to prepare, and means that by the time you perform a ritual, everything should feel familiar.

Obtaining a Promotion

You've been building your reputation at work, steadily working your way through the ranks, but you cannot progress to the next level. The promotion you dream of is elusive. After some reflection, you realize that this is largely because people see you as practical and effective, but they don't see you as leadership material.

Rather than working a ritual to influence others, you decide that the best way to proceed is to increase your personal sense of authority, so that others will perceive this quality within you. When you act as a leader, you are more likely to be promoted to a position that involves leadership.

After reading the descriptions of the angels in this book, you feel that working with Tzadkiel would be the most effective way to call forth a sense of personal authority. You decide that you will perform the ritual four times, once each Sunday, as that is convenient and feels like a good time.

On the first Sunday, you scan the letters and chant the angel's name, as instructed. You sense a presence, as though somebody else is in the room. You recognize that the angel Tzadkiel is present, and so you stop chanting and calmly state your request. You say, 'Tzadkiel, I ask that you give me a sense of authority. Help me to feel like a leader and act like a leader.' You ask this with sincerity, and you say *thank you* to Tzadkiel, thinking the angel's name while gazing at the sigil. You feel as though you are saying *thank you* for a wish that has already been fulfilled.

You take your mind off the magick, and spend the afternoon reading about leadership qualities. You decide to make one small change at work; you will actively choose to express your opinion during this week's Project Planning Meeting. It's not a massive step, but it is something, and you commit to it. That is enough for the magick to respond, and you begin to notice that leadership qualities arise in you. When others begin to see this in you, the promotion feels near.

You continue with the ritual for three more Sundays, because that is what you planned in advance, and after each ritual you plan more activities that contribute to the magick, taking steps to enact your newfound leadership qualities.

Recovering After a Major Project

You've been working on the release of a new product, and after months of development, feedback, market testing and countless other time-sapping activities, the day has come to actually release the product. This is a major step for your small business, and one that means a lot to you. But you also recognize that you are exhausted. You could wait until after the launch, once you know how sales are going, but the truth is, getting to this point was a major project in itself. If you're to be effective during the actual launch and promotion phase, you need to recover.

You study this book closely, and ascertain that Kumiel – Angel of Rejuvenation, could most likely help. Kumiel can restore your mental energy so that you no longer feel overwhelmed by what lies ahead. You decide that you will call on Kumiel just once, and ask sincerely for help with your exhaustion. That night you scan the letters and chant the angel's name, as instructed. After chanting for some time, you do not feel the angel's presence at all, but you know the ritual practice has effectively called the angel, and so you proceed to make your request.

You say, 'Kumiel, I ask that you renew my energy. Give me relief from this exhaustion, so that what lies ahead feels like a welcome challenge.' This is quite a specific request, but this is your sincere desire, and is worded clearly enough.

You complete the magick with your thanks, and the feeling that it has already been achieved. You contribute to the result by setting aside half an hour each day, where you will go down to your favorite park and just sit quietly, watching the world go by. This contribution helps to stimulate the magick into renewing your energy. Over the coming weeks, you notice a gradual increase in your energy levels, and the launch of the project does not overwhelm you.

Finding Clarity in a Relationship

The first few months of this relationship were pure joy, but now that things have settled a little, you feel confused. Yes, you feel like you're in love, but you find that your partner annoys you, makes you feel impatient. It could be that you're just not suited, or it could be that you're caving in to your familiar fear of commitment. It's impossible for you to know whether you're sabotaging the relationship, or having honest emotions of doubt.

After studying this book, you turn to Lahaviel – Angel of Sublimation, who can purify confused emotions and strip away illusions. Given that this is a complex and demanding situation, you decide to work this ritual once a day for eleven days.

You scan the letters and chant as instructed, and you feel a slight change in temperature, signifying the presence of the angel. You state your request. 'Lahaviel, I ask that you bring clarity to this relationship. Help me understand how I really feel.' You can name your partner if you wish, but it is not essential, as your thoughts, images and feelings communicate what you mean to the angel.

After you have given thanks, as though the problem is already solved, you contribute to the magick in several ways. Firstly, you decide to practice patience with your partner. If it fails, that's going to tell you something. You're also going to try being more honest, more open with your feelings. It might cause trouble, but it might lead to better communication. You also decide to spend some time each day talking to a friend about this relationship, to see if you can work out what's bothering you. You don't focus on what the magick is doing, but you do stay focused on the relationship.

Each day, you discover new thoughts and feelings, so each day you modify the request slightly. By the final day, you're fairly certain that you are in love, and that you've been sabotaging the relationship with your own fear. On the final day, you say, 'Lahaviel, let me feel the full extent of my love. If this is real, I want to feel it.' Lahaviel can purify and clarify emotions, so this request is in keeping with your overall request. You make sure that you contribute to this, by noticing your emotions, letting them arise clearly, staying as free of distraction as possible.

This magick is so personal that examples like these will only ever be a guideline. Your own experience may be quite different. As you can see, however, choosing an angel, setting a number of days, and committing to the change by enacting the change, is the best way to work in harmony with the angel.

The 42 Angels of Transformation

On the following pages you will find descriptions of the powers of the forty-two angels. These are, as explained earlier, quite brief, and sometimes abstract, but these descriptions are sufficient to guide your intuition regarding each angel. Take the time to read about the angels, and work out which powers appeal to you.

Beneath these you find the eight names and words of power that are used to grant access to the angel, and then the angel's name, spelt phonetically. On each subsequent page, you find the angel's sigil.

Orpaniel – Angel of Light

The angel Orpaniel is called when you need to deal with difficult emotions that occur due to relationships. The angel sheds light on these relationships, to bring healing.

Orpaniel can be used to heal a relationship that is damaged, but this works best when the relationship is fundamentally sound beneath that damage. If the relationship has been harmed by the surface problems of impatience, mistrust, complacency or other aspects of neglect, then the angel can help to restore the mutual appreciation and enjoyment of love.

Orpaniel can also ease the pain of a breakup, bringing you relief from your suffering and feelings of loss. This can be particularly useful when the loss is tied up with feelings of guilt and regret.

This angel can ease the pain of grief, when a loved one passes away. Although you do not want to forget a loved one, the pain can sometimes lead you into a place where you linger in morose feelings for too long. When you feel the need to recover from grief, the angel brings healing.

Orpaniel can restore friendship when that friendship has been damaged. Even when there is recent anger and disagreement, the angel can help to restore friendship.

ZAHD-KEY-ELL
UB-AH-GEE-TAHTZ
AH-DEER-EAR-AWE-TZ
BAH-HEAR-EAR-AWE-TZ
GUH-VEER-YAH-RAWN
YEEG-BAH-YAH
TUH-LAHM-YAH
TZ-TAHN-YAH

OAR-PAH-KNEE-ELL

The Sigil of Orpaniel

Boel – Angel of Truth

When you need to tell a difficult or painful truth, Boel can give you the strength to tell your highest truth. There are times when you know that you no longer want to keep a secret, but you fear the difficulty of expressing your truth. Work with this angel, and you will find the strength to tell the truth. This does not mean that others will always be pleased to hear what you say, but it does mean you will be understood as clearly as possible.

When you want to perceive truth in any situation, Boel can clarify and extend your perception. There are many times at work, in relationships or in business matters, when you simply can't tell what others are thinking. Boel can bring the clarity you seek.

ZAHD-KEY-ELL
UB-AH-GEE-TAHTZ
AH-DEER-EAR-AWE-TZ
BAH-HEAR-EAR-AWE-TZ
GUH-VEER-YAH-RAWN
YEEG-BAH-YAH
TUH-LAHM-YAH
TZ-TAHN-YAH

BAW-ELL

The Sigil of Boel

Gavriel – Angel of Strength

Gavriel provides strength by making you deeply aware of your own purpose, building your self-image and surety. You can call on the angel at any time when you need to access your personal strength, and you will receive assistance. But you can also work with Gavriel every few weeks, to build your strength continually. You may have met people who exude an air of calm and nobility. They appear strong, without boasting, bragging or swaggering. This is the style of strength that Gavriel can bestow upon you. It is a genuine inner strength, rather than bravado, and it increases your ability to face situations, and makes you more appealing to friends, family and lovers.

ZAHD-KEY-ELL
UB-AH-GEE-TAHTZ
AH-DEER-EAR-AWE-TZ
BAH-HEAR-EAR-AWE-TZ
GUH-VEER-YAH-RAWN
YEEG-BAH-YAH
TUH-LAHM-YAH
TZ-TAHN-YAH

GAHV-REE-ELL

The Sigil of Gavriel

Iophiel – Angel of Beauty

Iophiel brings more beauty to your creative work. Whether you write, paint, dance, sing, design, or work in any other art form, you can increase the depth of beauty in your work by calling on Iophiel. The angel inspires you by directing you to see what you already know, and to access the free and authentic aspects of your creativity. You can call on Iophiel to assist with your creative development over the coming years, or you can ask for assistance with a specific project or creation.

ZAHD-KEY-ELL
UB-AH-GEE-TAHTZ
AH-DEER-EAR-AWE-TZ
BAH-HEAR-EAR-AWE-TZ
GUH-VEER-YAH-RAWN
YEEG-BAH-YAH
TUH-LAHM-YAH
TZ-TAHN-YAH

EE-OH-FEE-ELL

The Sigil of Iophiel

Tumiel - Angel of Perfection

When you are stuck in blame, resentment or jealousy, call on Tumiel for release, to stop the negative emotions from eating away at you.

This angel can help you to see the perfection in those you love. By helping to undercover your unconditional love, you are led to find forgiveness for those who have wronged you. The angel does not blind you to the deeds that have been done, and indeed may give you more clarity than before, but removes the pain by easing you toward a loving forgiveness.

ZAHD-KEY-ELL
UB-AH-GEE-TAHTZ
AH-DEER-EAR-AWE-TZ
BAH-HEAR-EAR-AWE-TZ
GUH-VEER-YAH-RAWN
YEEG-BAH-YAH
TUH-LAHM-YAH
TZ-TAHN-YAH

TWO-ME-ELL

The Sigil of Tumiel

Tzadkiel – Angel of Authority

If you work with groups of people, and wish to be seen as a leader, call on Tzadkiel to increase your personal sense of authority. The angel can bring forth your innate strength and majesty, so that you are seen by others as a leader.

You can call on Tzadkiel to gradually increase your sense of majesty and authority over the coming months, or you can call for assistance during a specific meeting or occasion.

ZAHD-KEY-ELL
UB-AH-GEE-TAHTZ
AH-DEER-EAR-AWE-TZ
BAH-HEAR-EAR-AWE-TZ
GUH-VEER-YAH-RAWN
YEEG-BAH-YAH
TUH-LAHM-YAH
TZ-TAHN-YAH

TZAHD-KEY-ELL

The Sigil of Tzadkiel

Kavtziel – Angel of Gathering

Kavtziel is an angel who can assist you in social situations, by making you feel relaxed with yourself. The angel encourages you to connect with your true self, and to project yourself, so that you are authentic and self-assured in social situations. You can call on the angel over the months and years to gradually build your ability to work in social situations, or you can call for help when a specific and challenging social situation is on the horizon.

CAH-MAH-ELL
KUH-RAH-SUH-TAHN
KUH-DAHM-YAH
RUH-GAHR-YAH
REE-REE-AH
SHUH-GAH-YAH
TUH-LAHT-YAH
NUH-HAH-REE-YAH

KAHV-TZEE-ELL

The Sigil of Kavtziel

Ravchiel – Angel of Passion

This is not an angel of lust, but of joy, and the pleasure you feel from living life to the full. When you feel that your love of life has faded, call on this angel to renew your personal vigour. Sometimes you may find an increase in your appreciation of life, and at other times you will find that you are inspired to go to new places, meet new people and try new things. The angel knows what is most likely to connect you to a passionate existence, and helps guide you toward that future.

Ravchiel can also be called to increase the passion in a relationship. If you find that a relationship has become tired, call on Ravchiel to bring renewed heat to the partnership.

CAH-MAH-ELL
KUH-RAH-SUH-TAHN
KUH-DAHM-YAH
RUH-GAHR-YAH
REE-REE-AH
SHUH-GAH-YAH
TUH-LAHT-YAH
NUH-HAH-REE-YAH

RAHV-CHEE-ELL

The Sigil of Ravchiel

Oziel – Angel of Change

When you want to overcome a bad habit it can be extremely difficult, because habits nearly always provide some form of comfort or relief. Attaining change requires courage and commitment, as well as the strength to live without the comfort that was previously provided by the habit. In short, change is difficult, and breaking habits can be almost impossible. Call on Oziel to stimulate change, when you want to remove a habit from your life. Know that Oziel can provide the strength you need to undergo change, as well as stimulating your courage and commitment to the process of change.

CAH-MAH-ELL
KUH-RAH-SUH-TAHN
KUH-DAHM-YAH
RUH-GAHR-YAH
REE-REE-AH
SHUH-GAH-YAH
TUH-LAHT-YAH
NUH-HAH-REE-YAH

AWE-ZEE-ELL

The Sigil of Oziel

Shemshiel – Angel of Illumination

Shemshiel is an angel of efficiency, and can cast light on areas of your life that are more of a burden that you realize. If you find that you never have enough time, call on Shemshiel to illuminate the blockages in your life. You will find that you become aware of habits, practices and styles of work that are not working effectively for you. The angel will also give you the intuition to discover better ways of going about your daily life, and your work life, to get more done with less effort.

CAH-MAH-ELL
KUH-RAH-SUH-TAHN
KUH-DAHM-YAH
RUH-GAHR-YAH
REE-REE-AH
SHUH-GAH-YAH
TUH-LAHT-YAH
NUH-HAH-REE-YAH

SHEM-SHE-ELL

The Sigil of Shemshiel

Tofiel – Angel of Contentment

The angel of contentment does not make you satisfied with all life, but rather removes fear. If you find that a situation makes you afraid, call on Tofiel to remove the fear. When the fear is gone, you still have to face the situation at hand, but you will do so from a place of contentment.

This power applies to fear of the unknown, when you are worried about things that may or may not happen. If you are worried about a possible future, let Tofiel ease your fear.

The angel also works to reduce fear when you know that something unwanted is definitely going to happen. If you're going to be speaking in public, undergoing a medical procedure or performing any activity that makes you fearful, Tofiel can give you a calm sense of contentment.

CAH-MAH-ELL
KUH-RAH-SUH-TAHN
KUH-DAHM-YAH
RUH-GAHR-YAH
REE-REE-AH
SHUH-GAH-YAH
TUH-LAHT-YAH
NUH-HAH-REE-YAH

TAW-FEE-ELL

The Sigil of Tofiel

Nagriel – Angel of Proclamation

When you need to get a message across, call on Nagriel to empower your communication. The angel can assist you in finding the most effective way to communicate your message. You may be inspired to find new ways of communicating, or may find that your current skills are honed at precisely the right time.

Nagriel can also be called before you make a public speech, or perform before an audience. Whether your message is artistic or more straightforward, the angel can help to bring a harmonious sense of balance to your message, so that you perform with ease.

CAH-MAH-ELL
KUH-RAH-SUH-TAHN
KUH-DAHM-YAH
RUH-GAHR-YAH
REE-REE-AH
SHUH-GAH-YAH
TUH-LAHT-YAH
NUH-HAH-REE-YAH

NAH-GREE-ELL

The Sigil of Nagriel

Nachliel – Angel of Compassion

When you are suffering emotionally, call on Nachliel to obtain relief and release from the pain. The angel can put a healing hand on your heart, to ease emotional pain. The compassion of this angel can be quite overwhelming at times, with a clear and direct feeling of comfort.

RAH-FAH-ELL
NUH-GAHD-EE-CHAHSH
NEESH-MAH-REE-YAH
GUH-HAH-REE-YAH
DUH-HAH-REE-YAH
YUH-HAH-LEE-YAH
KASS-EE-YAH
SHEEG-YAWN-YAH

NAHCH-LEE-ELL

The Sigil of Nachliel

Gavoriel – Angel of Harmony

Finding harmony in a hectic life can be difficult. When you feel overwhelmed by a rush of difficult circumstances, call on Gavoriel to restore a sense of harmony. You will find that you are able to sense your own inner peace, even though the world around you may continue to speed ahead. The angel can even make it feel like time has slowed down for you, so that you are able to achieve more in less time, and remain close to a feeling of personal harmony.

The angel also helps restore harmony to a relationship that has become difficult, by bringing a calm sense of love to the surface. This can also apply to a household that has slipped into a period of discontent. Gavoriel can fill the home with a sense of peace and love that helps restore harmony.

RAH-FAH-ELL
NUH-GAHD-EE-CHAHSH
NEESH-MAH-REE-YAH
GUH-HAH-REE-YAH
DUH-HAH-REE-YAH
YUH-HAH-LEE-YAH
KASS-EE-YAH
SHEEG-YAWN-YAH

GAH-VAW-REE-ELL

The Sigil of Gavoriel

Dahniel – Angel of Balance

When your life feels out of balance, you can't always tell why. If you feel that your life is too stressful, too shallow, too busy, too boring, or extreme in any other way, call on Dahniel to reveal to you the source of the imbalance. The insights you gain may be quite unexpected, and can help you to restore a sense of balance in your life.

When you know where a source of imbalance lies, you can call on Dahniel to show you possible solutions. Say, for example, that you know you are working too hard, but you can't see a way to avoid this, call on Dahniel to reveal a pathway to a more balanced life. The solution may come in the form of intuition and revelation, or through new opportunities that make it easier for you to restore balance.

RAH-FAH-ELL
NUH-GAHD-EE-CHAHSH
NEESH-MAH-REE-YAH
GUH-HAH-REE-YAH
DUH-HAH-REE-YAH
YUH-HAH-LEE-YAH
KASS-EE-YAH
SHEEG-YAWN-YAH

DAH-KNEE-ELL

The Sigil of Dahniel

Yehodiel – Angel of Insight

The angel Yehodial can provide insight into current situations, to give you a better sense of perspective. Is this a situation that's going to affect the rest of your life, or is it something that appears worse than it is? Yehodiel helps reveal your inner relationships to the situation at hand, so that you gain a direct understanding of the significance of a current situation.

You can also call on Yehodiel when you are unsure about a change in a relationship. Whether the change comes from you, or the other person, you can ask Yehodiel to provide you with an insight into the relationship. The angel helps you to see how you relate to this situation, and will give you a strong intuition about how the relationship is likely to develop in the next few months.

RAH-FAH-ELL
NUH-GAHD-EE-CHAHSH
NEESH-MAH-REE-YAH
GUH-HAH-REE-YAH
DUH-HAH-REE-YAH
YUH-HAH-LEE-YAH
KASS-EE-YAH
SHEEG-YAWN-YAH

YEH-HAW-DEE-ELL

The Sigil of Yehodiel

Kevashiel – Angel of Surrender

When you want something desperately, there is the potential for your desperation to make your desire elusive, or at least to make your pursuit of that desire unpleasant. Call on Kevashiel to help you surrender to the situation. This is not about giving up, or letting things happen according to chance, but about finding a state of peace while events unfold. Your desires and your directed will to change the world remain in place, but you obtain a state of peace in the interim. This means that rather than being pestered by fear and doubts about your desire, you enter a state of calm expectation.

This power can be especially useful when you work with magick. When you use magick to obtain a desire, desperate and urgent need can prevent the magick from working. You can call on Kevashiel to ease your lust for a result, giving you a calm and accepting patience that makes the magick more likely to manifest. The more you work with this angel, the more effectively you can obtain the desired state of detachment from your need.

RAH-FAH-ELL
NUH-GAHD-EE-CHAHSH
NEESH-MAH-REE-YAH
GUH-HAH-REE-YAH
DUH-HAH-REE-YAH
YUH-HAH-LEE-YAH
KASS-EE-YAH
SHEEG-YAWN-YAH

KEH-VAH-SHE-ELL

The Sigil of Kevashiel

Shahariel - Angel of Connection

Shahariel can help you to appreciate the bond of love between yourself and another. When the value in a relationship has been concealed by bickering, arguments and mundane problems, this angel can help you to appreciate the genuine bond of love that exists. The angel helps to purify your connection to the other person. If you find that you are prone to being petty, distrustful or impatient, call on Shahariel to connect you to the genuine emotions that empower the relationship.

RAH-FAH-ELL
NUH-GAHD-EE-CHAHSH
NEESH-MAH-REE-YAH
GUH-HAH-REE-YAH
DUH-HAH-REE-YAH
YUH-HAH-LEE-YAH
KASS-EE-YAH
SHEEG-YAWN-YAH

SHAH-HAH-REE-ELL

The Sigil of Shahariel

Berachiel – Angel of Intuition

There are few skills as valuable as intuition, and you can call on Berachiel to improve your intuition. You can ask the angel to improve your overall intuition, and each time you make the request you will find an improvement. Make sure you start to trust your intuition, as your part of this work.

You can also request improved intuition related to a specific situation or person. If you find that your intuition feels clouded, ask Berachiel to improve your intuition regarding that person or situation, and you will find it easier to sense the truth of the situation.

HAH-KNEE-ELL
BUH-TAHR-TZAH-TAHG
BAW-AH-LEE-YAH
TAWD-AH-REE-YAH
RAH-ME-YAH
TZAHTZ-TZEE-YAH
TAH-HAH-VUH-HEE-AH
GAHL-GAH-LEE-YAH

BEH-RAH-CHEE-ELL

The Sigil of Berachiel

Tahftiel – Angel of Acceptance

Magick is partly about rejecting notions of fate or destiny, and choosing your own path. You guide your life through deliberate choice and acts of will. There are times, however, when accepting a situation is more important than fighting it, and this acceptance can bring great peace and happiness.

Your first job is to discern whether or not acceptance is the best path. If you are facing a difficult situation, call on Tahftiel to give you clarity. Ask if this is a situation you should accept, or whether it is something you can genuinely fight. The answer may come in the form of intuition, signs and omens, or a moment of certainty, and the answer may come in a rush or gradually, over weeks. The angel looks deep into your heart, and sees the potential of the situation, perceiving the outcome that is most likely to bring you happiness.

If you discover that you can persist on your current path, do so. If not, call on Tahftiel to help you accept and let go. When you are deeply entwined with a person or situation, moving on can be a huge challenge, but this angel will give you the courage and wisdom to accept the change, giving you the opportunity to deliberately shape your future.

HAH-KNEE-ELL
BUH-TAHR-TZAH-TAHG
BAW-AH-LEE-YAH
TAWD-AH-REE-YAH
RAH-ME-YAH
TZAHTZ-TZEE-YAH
TAH-HAH-VUH-HEE-AH
GAHL-GAH-LEE-YAH

TAHF-TEE-ELL

The Sigil of Tahftiel

Rachmiel – Angel of Tenderness

Rachmiel is an angel of affection and tenderness, and can be called upon to renew these aspects of a relationship. If you feel that you have hardened in relation to a lover or family member, Rachmiel can ease your cynicism and return you to a state of warm affection.

HAH-KNEE-ELL
BUH-TAHR-TZAH-TAHG
BAW-AH-LEE-YAH
TAWD-AH-REE-YAH
RAH-ME-YAH
TZAHTZ-TZEE-YAH
TAH-HAH-VUH-HEE-AH
GAHL-GAH-LEE-YAH

RAHCH-MEE-ELL

The Sigil of Rachmiel

Tzafuniel – Angel of Endurance

Within us all is strength and resilience, and the ability to keep going in the face of extreme odds and exhaustion. At times like these, you can call on Tzafuniel to access the depths of your personal endurance, so that you can get through a difficult time or see a project through to completion.

      This angel can also help to improve your ability to be patient. If you find that you are undermining a situation with impatience, call on Tzafuniel to give you a calm patience.

HAH-KNEE-ELL
BUH-TAHR-TZAH-TAHG
BAW-AH-LEE-YAH
TAWD-AH-REE-YAH
RAH-ME-YAH
TZAHTZ-TZEE-YAH
TAH-HAH-VUH-HEE-AH
GAHL-GAH-LEE-YAH

TZAH-FOO-KNEE-ELL

The Sigil of Tzafuniel

Trumiel – Angel of Exaltation

Trumiel can ensure that you are seen in a good light by others in your workplace, family or social group. If you feel that you are seen as lowly, or an outsider, this angel can help to make you raise your profile and be seen in a good light.

You can also call on Trumiel to ease loneliness by helping you make new friends. If you move to a new area, start new work, or find that your social life closes up, call on Trumiel to open your reality to the potential of new friendship.

HAH-KNEE-ELL
BUH-TAHR-TZAH-TAHG
BAW-AH-LEE-YAH
TAWD-AH-REE-YAH
RAH-ME-YAH
TZAHTZ-TZEE-YAH
TAH-HAH-VUH-HEE-AH
GAHL-GAH-LEE-YAH

TRUE-ME-ELL

The Sigil of Trumiel

Gedodiel – Angel of Sanctuary

When you feel the need to withdraw from the world for a while, call on Gedodiel to give you sanctuary. You will find it easier to find the space and time to reflect on yourself, your needs and your creative work. This applies whether you need a few days, or an extended period of time.

Gedodiel also helps if you need to find peace when surrounded by turmoil. If you are in the middle of a hectic life, or a difficult family situation, connecting with Gedodiel can help you find inner sanctuary, so that you stay in touch with who you are, and remain impervious to the distractions caused by other people.

HAH-KNEE-ELL
BUH-TAHR-TZAH-TAHG
BAW-AH-LEE-YAH
TAWD-AH-REE-YAH
RAH-ME-YAH
TZAHTZ-TZEE-YAH
TAH-HAH-VUH-HEE-AH
GAHL-GAH-LEE-YAH

GEH-DAW-DEE-ELL

The Sigil of Gedodiel

Cheziel – Angel of Visions

The angel Cheziel can be called on to bring visions, when you require insight into a specific situation. This angel will not make you somebody who generally has visions, but if there is something you need to know, the angel can help. It is usually wise to collect facts, notice signs and be aware of your intuition, in any given situation, but sometimes you want a rush of information or insight that can fuel your decisions. Such visions can be a great source of mystical guidance. To achieve such visions, call on this angel immediately before entering a state of meditation, or before sleep if you wish the visions to come to you in dreams.

The extent to which you will experience these visions depends partly upon your natural ability in this area, as well as your ability to let go and allow such images to arise. If you are new to this, don't be put off. For some, the angel can release visions with extreme ease. Others may only catch a hint of a vision, or a slight sense of the images and feelings that exist beyond the obvious surface of things. Persistence and repetition is the key to unlocking this power.

ME-CHAH-ELL
CHUH-KAHB-TAH-NAH
CHEEN-AHN-AH-YAH
KAH-TAH-KAH-YAH
BUH-HAH-VUH-HAH-VUH-YAH
TAH-VUH-HAW-YAH
NUH-TAH-NEE-YAH
AH-MAH-MAH-YAH

CHEH-ZEE-ELL

The Sigil of Cheziel

Kumiel – Angel of Rejuvenation

Kumiel is an angel of personal rejuvenation, especially in areas of mental energy and communication.

If you are weary from overwork, stress or any other factor that has brought mental exhaustion, call on Kumiel to renew your energy.

When communication breaks down, due to exhaustion or apathy, this angel can invigorate the communication. Let the angel know who is involved in such communication, naming them specifically. If you find that all your communications suffer, you can ask for a general rejuvenation of your ability to communicate.

ME-CHAH-ELL
CHUH-KAHB-TAH-NAH
CHEEN-AHN-AH-YAH
KAH-TAH-KAH-YAH
BUH-HAH-VUH-HAH-VUH-YAH
TAH-VUH-HAW-YAH
NUH-TAH-NEE-YAH
AH-MAH-MAH-YAH

KOO-ME-ELL

The Sigil of Kumiel

Barkiel – Angel of Lightning

Barkiel is an angel of mental alertness, intellect and inspired thought. You call on this angel when you need to think clearly, intuitively and with great intelligence. This can be useful when working on a creative project, or when preparing for (or taking) an exam. If you are involved in a work project that is taxing your capabilities, call on this angel to help release your innate intelligence.

Barkiel can also assist with rapid communication. When you want others to hear you, and understand what you have to say, call on this angel. This can be useful before a presentation, when launching a project, or when talking over something important in a relationship. Communication is more difficult than ever, in an age of information noise, so call on this angel to get your message through.

ME-CHAH-ELL
CHUH-KAHB-TAH-NAH
CHEEN-AHN-AH-YAH
KAH-TAH-KAH-YAH
BUH-HAH-VUH-HAH-VUH-YAH
TAH-VUH-HAW-YAH
NUH-TAH-NEE-YAH
AH-MAH-MAH-YAH

BAR-KEY-ELL

The Sigil of Barkiel

Tahariel – Angel of Purification

Tahariel can purify your thoughts and emotional state, removing negative energies that cause confusion, fear or despair.

When your thoughts are being led by negative emotions, call on this angel to clarify your emotional state. By lessening the impact of painful emotions and negative thoughts, your thinking should become brighter, more precise, and led by your true desires rather than your fears.

If a situation is causing you undue fear, which seems too extreme for the circumstances, call on Tahariel to ease your suffering. The angel can lessen fear that comes without apparent logical cause.

ME-CHAH-ELL
CHUH-KAHB-TAH-NAH
CHEEN-AHN-AH-YAH
KAH-TAH-KAH-YAH
BUH-HAH-VUH-HAH-VUH-YAH
TAH-VUH-HAW-YAH
NUH-TAH-NEE-YAH
AH-MAH-MAH-YAH

TAH-HAH-REE-ELL

The Sigil of Tahariel

Nuriel – Angel of Splendour

Nuriel can restore your confidence in yourself and your abilities. When you are filled with doubt about yourself, your purpose and what you can contribute to the world, ask Nuriel to give you confidence. The results will build in the days and weeks that follow the ritual.

If you are about to embark on a specific venture that requires confidence, such as a business proposal, a public speaking event, or a large social occasion, you can call for Nuriel to stand with you, and provide you with the confidence you need to be relaxed in such a situation.

ME-CHAH-ELL
CHUH-KAHB-TAH-NAH
CHEEN-AHN-AH-YAH
KAH-TAH-KAH-YAH
BUH-HAH-VUH-HAH-VUH-YAH
TAH-VUH-HAW-YAH
NUH-TAH-NEE-YAH
AH-MAH-MAH-YAH

NOO-REE-ELL

The Sigil of Nuriel

Amiel – Angel of Charm

Amiel can assist you in becoming the most charming and attractive version of yourself. Call on this angel to help you access your raw sexual charisma, and make that inner charm be seen by those you encounter.

You can call on Amiel to assist with confidence, so that you feel more relaxed when talking to people that you find attractive.

ME-CHAH-ELL
CHUH-KAHB-TAH-NAH
CHEEN-AHN-AH-YAH
KAH-TAH-KAH-YAH
BUH-HAH-VUH-HAH-VUH-YAH
TAH-VUH-HAW-YAH
NUH-TAH-NEE-YAH
AH-MAH-MAH-YAH

AH-MEE-ELL

The Sigil of Amiel

Yisrael – Angel of Imagination

Call on Yisrael to improve your imagination. You may want to improve your ability to visualize, for the purpose of certain magickal practices. Or you may want your imagination to be stronger, to aid your creative work. The focus here is not only on the visual imagination, but also the ability to imagine that which has not yet come into being. For creative people, and those who would change the world, the ability to imagine anew is vital.

You can also call on Yisrael to guide your imagination directly, when working on a specific project or artwork. When starting out, and pondering the possibilities, ask for your imagination to be unleashed, so that you can imagine on a scale that would not have been possible before.

GAH-BREE-ELL
YUH-GAHL-PUH-ZAHK
YUH-HAHL-SHU-RAH-YAH
GAWD-EAR-AH-YAH
LUH-MEEM-AH-REE-YAH
PUH-CORK-AH-REE-YAH
ZAH-RAH-EE-YAH
KUH-MAH-LEE-YAH

YEES-RAH-ELL

The Sigil of Yisrael

Gahdiel – Angel of Intent

The angel Gahdiel can help provide the motivation to apply yourself to a goal or intention. When you intend to achieve something, but find yourself bound by idleness or despair, this angel can galvanize your intentions, helping you find the energy and commitment to work consistently on your goals and dreams. When a creative project falters, for example, this angel can help you to find the commitment to see it through.

You can also call on Gahdiel to make your intentions easier to achieve. When you sense that obstacles are scattered on your path, call on Gahdiel to remove those obstacles, so that your intentions can be realized.

GAH-BREE-ELL
YUH-GAHL-PUH-ZAHK
YUH-HAHL-SHU-RAH-YAH
GAWD-EAR-AH-YAH
LUH-MEEM-AH-REE-YAH
PUH-CORK-AH-REE-YAH
ZAH-RAH-EE-YAH
KUH-MAH-LEE-YAH

GAH-DEE-ELL

The Sigil of Gahdiel

Lahaviel – Angel of Sublimation

Lahaviel has the power to purify confused emotions. If you feel baffled by your wants and needs, confused about what you want or uncertain how you really feel about somebody or a situation, call on this angel. By stripping away illusions, the angel can make your pure feelings more apparent, and this can be a source of genuine guidance.

GAH-BREE-ELL
YUH-GAHL-PUH-ZAHK
YUH-HAHL-SHU-RAH-YAH
GAWD-EAR-AH-YAH
LUH-MEEM-AH-REE-YAH
PUH-CORK-AH-REE-YAH
ZAH-RAH-EE-YAH
KUH-MAH-LEE-YAH

LAH-HAH-VEE-ELL

The Sigil of Lahaviel

Pahniel – Angel of Presence

Pahniel is an angel that can make your presence more noticeable to others. This is ideal at times when you want to shine, to be seen and to project yourself outward. Whether you a promoting yourself, a product, a project or simply wanting to be popular in a crowd, Pahniel works to make others sense your presence.

Pahniel is a subtle angel, and does not make others flock to you in awe, but projects the authenticity of your presence, so that others sense and recognize what is good and worthwhile about you. This is an angel to call on when you want others to see what you genuinely have to offer.

Although the power is described in terms of how others see you, be aware that this magick is more about extending the warmth and intensity of your presence, rather than directly influencing others. When your presence is projected warmly, it is impossible for others not to notice, and in sensing your warmth, people may be more receptive to your thoughts and ideas.

GAH-BREE-ELL
YUH-GAHL-PUH-ZAHK
YUH-HAHL-SHU-RAH-YAH
GAWD-EAR-AH-YAH
LUH-MEEM-AH-REE-YAH
PUH-CORK-AH-REE-YAH
ZAH-RAH-EE-YAH
KUH-MAH-LEE-YAH

PAH-KNEE-ELL

The Sigil of Pahniel

Zachriel - Angel of Instigation

This angel brings about change. When you want to stir up your reality, to make change more likely, you call on Zachriel. This can lead to new opportunities, chance meetings and surprise events that can influence your future.

You can ask the angel to stir up your reality in this way, whenever you are trying to start over, push ahead with a project, or make a big change in your life. By loosening the grip that habit and stability have on your life, you make changes far more likely. Rather than directing the magick at a specific situation, you ask that your entire reality be made more changeable, and then subsequently direct your personal efforts at the life areas where you want to see change.

Be aware that this angel will cause change in your life, which means there will be some disruption of normality. The angel will not cause chaos, or turn your life upside down, but remember that change can be uncomfortable at first. If you ask for change, know that change will come. Welcome the changes, and know that this magick doesn't unravel your life, but makes you open to transformation that can lead to a better future.

GAH-BREE-ELL
YUH-GAHL-PUH-ZAHK
YUH-HAHL-SHU-RAH-YAH
GAWD-EAR-AH-YAH
LUH-MEEM-AH-REE-YAH
PUH-CORK-AH-REE-YAH
ZAH-RAH-EE-YAH
KUH-MAH-LEE-YAH

ZAHCH-REE-ELL

The Sigil of Zachriel

Kedoshiel – Angel of Integrity

The angel Kedoshiel can help you maintain your integrity when others try to make you compromise. If you are struggling with the demands of others, who would seek to limit your work, your life, or your creativity, call for the assistance of Kedoshiel.

The angel will not remove all obstacles, but will connect you more deeply to your true feelings, making it easier for you to continue with your life. Others will sense your power, your authority and the intensity of your integrity. This can make it easier for you to assert yourself in any situation.

You can ask the angel to grant you a general air of authority that comes from your personal integrity, which can help to guide you through the following weeks and months. Alternatively, you can ask for this power to be directed to a particular situation that is causing problems.

GAH-BREE-ELL
YUH-GAHL-PUH-ZAHK
YUH-HAHL-SHU-RAH-YAH
GAWD-EAR-AH-YAH
LUH-MEEM-AH-REE-YAH
PUH-CORK-AH-REE-YAH
ZAH-RAH-EE-YAH
KUH-MAH-LEE-YAH

KEH-DAW-SHE-ELL

The Sigil of Kedoshiel

Shelgiel – Angel of Brilliance

Shelgiel can turn night into day, and illuminate the darkness within you. That is to say, this angel can guide you to understand your desires more clearly. When you feel confused, uncertain of your direction, or baffled by who you are and where you are going, this angel can help you to know what it is that you truly want. Call on Shelgiel to unravel the mystery of yourself, and you will gain insights into the desires that you need to fulfil. These may be earthy desires, or a yearning for the spiritual.

SAHN-DAHL-FAWN
SHUH-KAHV-TZUH-YAHT
SHAH-TUH-HAWD-RAH-YAH
KAH-DAWSH-YAH
VUH-HAH-HAH-LAY-LEE-YAH
TZ-AH-DEE-YAH
YEET-HAH-DREE-YAH
TAHM-TAIL-EE-YAH

SHELL-GEE-ELL

The Sigil of Shelgiel

Karviel – Angel of Unfolding

The angel Karviel has the power to let a situation unfold at great speed. This means that you can let a situation reach its maximum potential in a much shorter time. This can help you see the true potential of a relationship, creative project, business venture or any other situation that you expect to develop over the coming months. Within a short time, you should see the situation change in a way that indicates whether it has a future, or whether it will in fact fade from your life.

Using this magick requires some courage. It should be used when you want a definite answer. Ask the angel to help the situation develop rapidly, in a way that reveals its maximum potential. In a relationship, you may find that things develop in a positive way, showing you that there is a great potential for the future. Or you may find that the relationship reaches its peak rapidly and begins to fade. In creative work, you may find that your ideas unfold rapidly, and this may lead you to see that there is potential in them. Or that they are more limited than you first hoped. In business, a potential change or new idea may reveal itself to have enormous potential, or may uncover its flaws clearly.

SAHN-DAHL-FAWN
SHUH-KAHV-TZUH-YAHT
SHAH-TUH-HAWD-RAH-YAH
KAH-DAWSH-YAH
VUH-HAH-HAH-LAY-LEE-YAH
TZ-AH-DEE-YAH
YEET-HAH-DREE-YAH
TAHM-TAIL-EE-YAH

CAR-VEE-ELL

The Sigil of Karviel

Vaviel – Angel of Fascination

Vaviel can create an aura of fascination, so that others are deeply charmed by your genuine presence. This is not a power that can fool people into liking you, because it encourages a genuine fascination. By making the brightest parts of you shine, while offering glimmers of your depths, it makes you a truly engaging person, that people want to know. Ask the angel for this power only if you want to be truly known by those who see you this way.

You can ask that the angel makes you generally fascinating, so that you will charm many that you meet, or to direct this fascination at one particular individual. Whether you want to attract genuine friendship or love, be aware that those who are fascinated by you will seek out your deepest truth, so be prepared to reveal the depths of your soul.

When you are fascinated by another, Vaviel can help to clarify your perception, so that you are able to see what is genuine, and what you may have invented through infatuation. In the early stages of a relationship, you may find it useful to obtain a clear perception of the person that fascinates you.

SAHN-DAHL-FAWN
SHUH-KAHV-TZUH-YAHT
SHAH-TUH-HAWD-RAH-YAH
KAH-DAWSH-YAH
VUH-HAH-HAH-LAY-LEE-YAH
TZ-AH-DEE-YAH
YEET-HAH-DREE-YAH
TAHM-TAIL-EE-YAH

VAH-VEE-ELL

The Sigil of Vaviel

Tzuriel – Angel of Pleasure

If you are overcome with the efforts of your earthly life, and need to indulge in pleasure, without guilt, this angel can bring you a taste of the good life. Call on the angel to bring you the relief of pleasure, and let the angel decide how you will taste these delights. You may be rewarded with unexpected travel, companionship, or some other opportunity. The results aren't always objectively spectacular, but the angel will respond with an opportunity that is attainable, when and where you need it. In some cases, that might just be an invitation to an unexpected event, or you may wander into an unexpectedly pleasant place where you find inspiration. In other cases, everything may unfold to bring you something more spectacular. This is quite an obscure power, but it works if you remain open minded.

Tzuriel can also help you find the spiritual in worldly pleasures. If you are travelling, taking a break, or simply indulging in good food and good times, call on the angel to help you understand more about yourself and your life through those pleasures. Again, this is quite an obscure power, but one that should not be dismissed, as it has enormous potential.

SAHN-DAHL-FAWN
SHUH-KAHV-TZUH-YAHT
SHAH-TUH-HAWD-RAH-YAH
KAH-DAWSH-YAH
VUH-HAH-HAH-LAY-LEE-YAH
TZ-AH-DEE-YAH
YEET-HAH-DREE-YAH
TAHM-TAIL-EE-YAH

TZOO-REE-ELL

The Sigil of Tzuriel

Ialpiel – Angel of Sustenance

Ialpiel gives you the power to be nourished by experience, rather than drained. If you feel that you are low on energy, or that the burdens of life take more from you than they give, call on Ialpiel. This angel can lift the weariness, and give sustenance. The burdens of life seem less, and you are able to feel strong even in difficult times.

SAHN-DAHL-FAWN
SHUH-KAHV-TZUH-YAHT
SHAH-TUH-HAWD-RAH-YAH
KAH-DAWSH-YAH
VUH-HAH-HAH-LAY-LEE-YAH
TZ-AH-DEE-YAH
YEET-HAH-DREE-YAH
TAHM-TAIL-EE-YAH

EE-AHL-PEE-ELL

The Sigil of Ialpiel

Tavriel – Angel of Completion

When you begin a project, and feel overwhelmed, Tavriel can give you the vision and persistence required to see the project through to completion.

If you are close to completing a project, but losing the will to continue, the angel can help you reach the finish line. Whether you're trying to pass an exam or start a business, Tavriel can offer the energy of completion, to guide you through the remaining stages of the project.

Tavriel can help you see what is of value and what can be discarded. When you are working on a large project, call on Tavriel to give you clarity about what is really required. You will gain insights into what should be preserved, or expanded, and what should be removed in order for you project to flourish. This might apply to writing a novel, buying a house, starting a business, or managing a large number of people. Any time you are trying to complete a large project, let its completion be guided by your perception of what needs to be preserved, and what can be discarded.

SAHN-DAHL-FAWN
SHUH-KAHV-TZUH-YAHT
SHAH-TUH-HAWD-RAH-YAH
KAH-DAWSH-YAH
VUH-HAH-HAH-LAY-LEE-YAH
TZ-AH-DEE-YAH
YEET-HAH-DREE-YAH
TAHM-TAIL-EE-YAH

TAHV-REE-ELL

The Sigil of Tavriel

Pronunciation Guide

When you first see the various angelic names and words of power, you may wonder whether you'll be able to say them correctly. You can trust me when I say that this book is absolutely Pronunciation Proof. You scan the letters visually, so you don't need to get the pronunciation perfectly correct.

Speak the words in capitals as though they are English. So you may see a word such as Adirirotz, which is pronounced as:

AH-DEER-EAR-AWE-TZ

This is one word, made up from five sounds. You read the sounds as though they are English. That would be as follows:

AH. The first sound is just the word *ah*.

DEER is the word *deer*.

EAR is the word *ear*.

AWE is the word *awe*.

TZ is the sound you get at the end of words such as *cats*, *bats* and *rats*.

Run these together and you get AH-DEER-EAR-AWE-TZ.

As you can see, it is quite easy to work out how to say the sounds, by finding an English equivalent.

It's worth looking at some of the more commonly used sounds in this book, to make sure you get them right. If these are even close to being correct, you'll be doing a great job.

UH

UH is *up* without the *p*. So if you see the sound **GUH**, you know that it sounds like *gut* without the *t*. **KUH** it like *cut* without the *t*.

AH

The **AH** sound is like the *ah* you get in *ma* and *pa*. When you say *ma* without the *m*, you've got the right sound.

Some words have **AH** in the middle. So **DAHM** is *ah* with *d* at the front and *m* and at the end. **GAHR** is the *ah* sound with *g* at the front and *r* at the end.

YAH

YAH is included in most of these words, so please note that **YAH** is, of course, *ah* with *y* at the front.

EH

EH is like the middle part of the word *net*. Say *net* without the *n* or the *t* and you've got **EH**.

AW

AW is like *awe*, or *raw* without the *r*. So if you see **HAWD**, you know it sounds like the word *awe* with *h* at the beginning and *d* at the end.

G

G sounds like the *g* in *give*, rather than the *g* in *gem*. So **GAH** sounds like the first part of *garlic*, (before you get to the r).

TZ

TZ is like the end of the word *cats*. Say *cats* out loud, then say *cats* without *ca* and you've got the right sound.

CH

Authentic Hebrew often uses the *ch* sound that you hear in the Scottish word *loch*, or the German *achtung*. You can study YouTube videos of native speakers using these words, to learn the *ch* sound. Alternatively, you can simply make a *k* sound when you see **CH**.

To illustrate this, you may have seen the name Ravchiel, which is pronounced as: RAHV-CHEE-ELL

CHEE is made with the CH sound discussed above, followed by EE. But if you struggle with that, simply replace every CH with a K. So that would make this RAHV-KEY-ELL. You may find that easier.

It is perfectly safe to practice the words before you actually come to perform the ritual, and I would recommend that you take the time to do this, so you can feel relaxed about the ritual itself.

The information above is all you need to get the pronunciations you need. It may take you a few minutes to work out the exact pronunciation that feels comfortable to you. This is time well spent, because learning the name in this way opens up yours sense of affinity to the angel.

By reaching for a pronunciation that feels right, you are already reaching out to the angel. By going through this process you connect yourself to the angel before you even say the name in a ritual. This is far more useful than an audio guide that you could mimic, so please take the time to work out the pronunciation that feels right. Remember, it doesn't have to be objectively correct, or perfect, so long as you follow these guidelines and find something that sounds right to you.

The Evocation of Angels

When you call a spirit to appear before you, it is generally known as evocation. Invocation, by contrast, is a process where you let the attributes, presence and powers of a spirit pass through you and be a part of you, for the duration of the ritual.

Evocation is about calling a spirit to appear before you, while remaining separate from you. Invocation is seen as a way of letting the spirit co-exist with you. Whatever you call it, the process described in this book is a blend of these two processes, but I prefer to think of it as an evocation.

Sometimes the terms evocation and invocation are used interchangeably, and at other times people use these words to mean very specific things. Some people insist that you *evoke* demons to appear (because invocation is too dangerous when it comes to demons), but that you only ever *invoke* an angel, because they are too holy to be evoked. To some, evocation is the act of calling a spirit that remains entirely separate from you, observed and seen, but not experienced, while invocation is largely an inner process, without you having to see the spirit.

I have found the distinction between evocation and invocation less and less important as the years go by. When I evoke a spirit of any kind, I consider it most successful if I experience the presence, atmosphere and power quality of the spirit, making it more like invocation. Equally, although the invocation of angels is pleasant, it can be useful to evoke them to visual appearance, where contact is direct. In short, I use magickal methods to call on spirits in an experience that feels like invocation, while retaining the immediacy and visual nature of an evocation. That is what you get in this part of the book.

One reason that I don't like to go into theory and definitions is that you very quickly come up against dogma, tradition, rules, opinions and all sorts of waffle that has very little to do with the practice of contacting a spirit. If you have a very strong opinion about this, based on your previous occult experience, please stick to your beliefs. I am not trying to convince you of anything, but forgive me if what I offer here is less than traditional. If you have no preconceived notions, that's also ok. What I'll show you here is a way to evoke an angel into your presence, with a deep, emotional, spiritual and intellectual connection to that angel. I will refer to this, quite simply, as evocation.

There are many ways to evoke spirits, and they range from basic chants through to full ceremonies that involve cleansing, confession, extensive ritual performance with robes and daggers, and so on. I have taken part in many types of magickal evocation, and I have found most of them to be rewarding. Although the efforts involved didn't always pay off, I enjoyed the process, and at the time, I even enjoyed the paraphernalia, costumes and dramatics. Now, I prefer to approach this with a method that is as simple and reliable as possible. I am more interested in the connection than I am in the trappings of the ritual.

It is true that the dramatic elements of ceremonial magick can make things feel more magickal. They can get you in the mood. But they are not guarantee of success. The most elaborate ritual I was ever involved in was an abject failure. I was in a very magickal space, and it felt like anything was possible, but despite the intense preparation and build-up, nothing happened. No presence was felt and no result was obtained. This is not altogether surprising. When you evoke a spirit you are attempting something so far from mainstream experience, that it would cause most people to assume that you are, to some extent, insane. If you achieve your aim, and see a spirit before you that, according to conventional science is not actually there, there are many people who would say you *have* crossed over to insanity. I believe that you can remain in perfect mental health when working this magick, but it's worth taking a moment to realise that you are attempting to achieve a mental state that is very far removed from normality. Do not expect it to be predictable or consistent.

The method presented here is not as obviously magickal as some. It lacks the candles and incense and wands that you will find in other procedures, but that's not to say those things are without value. The reason that people wear the costumes of their professions is that it is easier to have the experience of being a lawyer, a doctor or captain if you feel like one, if you feel convincing and authentic in your costume.

Some people find that dressing in a certain way, being outdoors at night, or using candles and so on, is the key that makes things feel magickal. If you find that using incense, and a circle of crystals and a room full of little waxy flames gets you in the mood for magick, then go ahead and create your own process. But be assured that these things are not essential. They are optional, for those who feel the need. Many people will find that following the ritual process as described is enough to get that feeling of magick.

My advice is to try the magick, as written, but if you find yourself yearning for a little more paraphernalia, go ahead and get what you need, but know that this is only a form of dressing up, to put you in the right mood. Being in the right mood can be a pathway into magickal evocation. My hope is that the ritual itself, when carried out with great diligence, will create the sensation of magick for you.

The Experience of Evocation

There are many reasons to evoke, and I know from the messages I receive that many people are hungry for a genuinely supernatural experience. Although this curiosity is reasonable, I believe that evocation should be pursued as a means of attaining better communication and interaction with the angels. You should evoke an angel when you sincerely believe that the contact has the potential to improve your life.

Where tasking can bring results, evocation can give you a much richer relationship with the angel, where you effectively discuss the issues at hand, and discover more about yourself, your potential and the best way to progress. Sometimes evocation is all about this communication, with the angel helping you to see who you are, what you can do and how you can change. At other times, evocation involves you asking the angel for help, rather than just guidance. That is, you can task an angel directly, during evocation, and you are likely to get a sense of how the magick is going to unfold in your life.

It should be stressed from the outset that, although angels can guide, they do not rule you. They are called to give personal advice, and to guide your transformation, but they do not make the decisions for you. You always have the choice to ignore what you are told, store it for another day, or take the time to let it sink into your consciousness. I point this out because the experience of evocation can be quite intense, and if you feel an overwhelming love and joy when in the presence of an angel, it can be easy to lose sight of who you are, what you want and where you are going. Thankfully, the angels are not going to take advantage of this, but it can mean that you become enamoured with the experience of angelic contact. It is worth remembering that angels do not wish to be worshiped. When you evoke, angels will often tell you this plainly and directly, and will emphasize that the awe inspiring love that you feel emanating from them is a fragment of the divine.

As I have said many times in my life, it is not my place to discuss the reality or otherwise of the angels, nor discuss how the experience of evocation can be married to various religious backgrounds. What I can tell you is that these angels are evoked by people from many religions, as well as by agnostics, and even some open-minded atheists. That sounds strange, but it is true. There are many people who do not believe in God, as such, but who are able to connect with angels and sense what, to them, is the nature of the universe. Angelic contact is, in my opinion, an objectively real experience that occurs independently of a belief system, so long as one is open to the presence of the angels as though they are real. When approached with this open receptivity, the angels can make themselves known to you. This brief paragraph is an attempt to show that the experience of contact is always unique, and will be shaped by your background, your personality, your experience, and your innate connection to magick. It should also be said that belief is not important. Sceptical people can experience a full evocation, while those who have always believed in angels may find they only get a slight sense of angelic presence.

One evocation is never the same as another, and the range of experience is vast. For some, it may be little more than a vague sense of a presence. For others, the angel appears visibly and audibly, as though standing in the room and conversing. Others experience the process as something more like a dream or vision. Some sense emotion and intelligence, while some see lights or shadows and distortions in the air, or catch a scent or hear a sound.

Remember that evocation changes over time, so what you experience the first time or after several months of work, may not be the same as the experience you have years later. Evocation is the long game. Your initial results may be overwhelming, and then may become less intense. Or your initial results may feel like a failure, and that can be disappointing if you're hoping to glimpse something wonderful.

I like to compare this to happiness. I do not believe we are meant to be happy all the time at all costs. Although you will see that all my books cover the importance of gratitude and appreciation, this does not mean living in a fake delusion of forced glee. I believe that we are granted the full spectrum of emotions in order to gain insight into ourselves, and negative emotions are not negative so much as deeply communicative. Happiness comes and goes, and although we often try to get back to a state of being happy, other states remain a valid part of our emotional makeup. But the thing with happiness is that, just because it is elusive, or fades, or vanishes completely, that doesn't mean that I give up on it. I don't say, 'I tried happiness and it didn't work.' You know that happiness is a state that occurs. It comes, it goes. The same is true of evocation. If you try it, and don't get what you want, or if you get what you want and then find it more difficult, don't write it off as something that doesn't work. Evocation is part of your magickal experience and can always be with you, even if it doesn't work as predictably as you might want it to work. When you make evocation a part of your life, rather than a passing magickal exercise, the reality of evocation unfolds more readily.

Evocation is not easy. The instructions are simple enough, but this does not mean you can get results without dedication, focus and clarity of intent. With most of the magick we publish, if you follow the instructions (and that includes the instructions about choosing carefully, directing your magick where change is possible, and working on your ability to let go of desperation), the results are achieved quite easily. They may take time, but they happen. With evocation, you should know that everything *can* work first time, but it might also take a long time to get the experience you're looking for. Sticking with the practice of evocation when nothing happens is difficult. When it feels like a failure, why should you continue? It can feel foolhardy to persist with something that you begin to doubt. I do not want to promise that you will see an angel if you persist for years, but I do know many people who found this work difficult, and yet they eventually achieved a connection that worked. I make no promises, because successful evocation is dependent on your personal ability to wield magick as much as it is on any instruction I can give. But I will say that if you persist, and use this instruction with determined enthusiasm, you are stepping into a new reality. That is no small thing, and I do not think it is something you will ever regret.

Some people see evocation as a knack or skill, like juggling or riding a bike. It clicks, and then you've got it. I think that is fairly accurate, but feel it's a little more like lucid dreaming. When you try and try to have a lucid dream, it can be very difficult to achieve, because the more you try, the more elusive the dream is. If you happen to have a lucid dream, the excitement can cause you to wake up. The very enthusiasm that gives you the impulse to work at this undermines your efforts. When you give up on lucid dreaming and decide to just get a good night's sleep, you go to bed and that very night you have a completely mind-blowing lucid dream. That happened to me, and has happened to many others. And something similar happens with evocation.

So does this mean you're meant to try for years and then give up? Not really. It means that striving for the result is less important than doing the work without expectation. I suggest that you follow the instructions, exactly as set out, while allowing your personal process to be guided by intuition, and allow the results to occur in whatever way they occur.

Follow the instructions and know that it can and does work, and that the results can be visual, dramatic and life-changing. But expect nothing. Say to yourself before you begin that doing the ritual, doing your part and reaching out for angelic contact, is all you want to do. Whether or not there is a response is out of your hands, so there's no reason to waste your energy on that.

Imagine you are in a long distance relationship, and your lover is on the other side of the world, in an unpredictable job with a strange schedule which makes it difficult for the two of you to talk on a regular basis. You really want to make contact, so that night you plan to call. You choose a time when your lover is quite likely to be free. You make the call, hoping for the best, but there's no answer and you're filled with disappointment. Here's another approach. You call every night, at a slightly different time, knowing that sooner or later you'll get through. You don't call every five minutes or send pestering texts. You call on a regular basis, knowing that eventually you'll get to talk. And then, eventually, you do make contact, and it's wonderful.

Approach evocation like that. You make the call, knowing that it could be answered first time, but not minding if it doesn't happen just yet, because it will happen eventually.

Somebody close to me compares evocation to the act of learning to sing. Some people have strong, natural singing voices, and sing beautifully not long after they learn to talk. For others, singing does not come easily, and requires the slow building of listening skills as well as practice with the physical apparatus of the voice. During this time, the singing is not good. It sounds awful. *But the only way to get better at singing is to sing.* So rather than keeping quiet, you sing, knowing that you'll get the notes eventually. You try to enjoy blasting out your songs in the meantime, no matter how they sound.

You can approach evocation in a similar way. You do the work, you go through the process, knowing that every time you do it, you're getting better. If you've ever struggled with your singing voice, you'll know that it can take months of hitting dud notes before you notice any improvement in range or tone. The same can be true with evocation, but you will also find that developments happen all of a sudden, when you least expect them. When you put in the consistent work, change is inevitable.

I went through a period where the style of evocation explored in this book did not work well for me, and I worried that I needed to do more, work harder, perform other rituals to improve my power, work on my imagination and so on. But the extra effort didn't seem to make a difference. Eventually, I decided to evoke as though it was working every time. I assumed that the angel came when called, that the angel was listening, and even responding. I treated the evocation as successful regardless of my experience. If I couldn't hear or see the angel, that was down to me and it didn't really matter. This was the single most effective change I made. It meant that no ritual felt wasted. Even if I felt nothing, sensed nothing, I accepted that the angel was helping me, and was guiding me.

I knew this was a form of double-think, or deliberate self-deception for a greater purpose. I knew, deep down, that I wanted a real evocation, where I could see and hear the angel. But I was able to pretend to myself, quite convincingly, that it didn't matter what the experience was like. Of course, if I'd done that for five years, it would be ludicrous to call those evocations successful – I'd just be fooling myself. But by carrying the ritual out without feeling needy or desperate, I did far more good than if I'd tried to will the evocation into working.

It would be misleading to say that those evocations were genuinely as effective as more direct evocation, but they were not wasted. I now believe that the angels do come when called, and if an evocation 'fails' it is merely because we are not currently open to seeing or hearing the angel. Rather than giving up, you persist until the experience returns.

I am not trying to prepare you for failure. It may seem that this chapter is aimed at lowering your expectations, but that is not my intention, and you should know this evocation method works, and I expect it to work quickly and easily for many people. But evocation is a fragile magick, and I am not going to say that the instructions given here are enough to guarantee success. They are enough to open the doorway to evocation. You may have to find your own way through that door.

Your first evocation might be completely successful. If so, you probably want to know what that's going to be like. As I've already indicated, the experience is so personal and so varied that it is almost impossible to summarise. You may sense a presence, feel an emotion, sense intelligence and might. You could see the angel in your imagination, or standing in the room. There may be flashes of light, soft voices or distant music. Many of these effects occur in the opening phase. The purpose of evocation is to communicate, so the state you are aiming for is more stable, where the presence you have called is tangible in some way. Again, this could mean that you see an angel standing in the room, or it may mean that you hear answers to your questions. It may just be that you are guided by emotions, hunches and a sense of guided inspiration. It is probably not useful to talk about the experience in much more detail. The point of this magick is to experience evocation rather than to theorise about it. I will guide you into the experience and you should let that experience be your own.

The Affinity Process

The practice I use for evoking the angels in this book is called The Affinity Process. In a following chapter I reveal the Evocation Keys for each angel. These Evocation Keys are short descriptions of the angels' appearance and presence, and by working with these impressions, you are able to forge a connection to the angel. Through the ritual of The Affinity Process, which employs the Evocation Keys, you call the angel into your presence. From there, you can speak to the angel directly, obtaining insights, wisdom or asking for change.

Before you begin, ensure that you have studied everything that comes before this chapter. Without adequate preparation, thorough reading and calm contemplation of the angels, you will stand little chance of success. Rush in, and you will be disappointed. Take the time to acquaint yourself with the preparatory techniques, and you should be able to make some form of contact with the angel.

This chapter, although potentially profound, is relatively brief. Do not mistake brevity for a lack of depth. Do not assume that these instructions can be carried out without a sincere commitment to the magick.

To achieve evocation, you do the following:

Choose an Angel

Choose an angel that is appropriate to your needs, or an angel that you feel a particular affinity to. When working with the tasking process, you may find that one angel works particularly well, or that you feel a strong connection. This is a good choice for evocation. If no particular angel stands out, then read thoroughly, and choose an angel that feels right to you, and one that has powers that appeal to you.

Become aware of the angel's Evocation Keys. In this example, we will say that you have been working with Iophiel on a creative project. During the task-based magick, you felt that Iophiel was aware of you. The magick worked well, and now you want to obtain more direct information. Iophiel is a good choice, so you look at the Evocation Keys.

You will read that, 'Iophiel appears in sapphire blue robes, against a pale blue sky. White blossom falls through the air. There is the floral scent of blossom. The angel conveys a feeling of love and courage.' You do not need to visualize these keys in any great detail at this point, but become familiar with them. When you use the Evocation Keys later in the ritual, they should seem very familiar, rather than in any way surprising. This only needs to take a few minutes.

Contemplate Purpose

Contemplate the purpose of the contact you wish to achieve. This may take a few minutes, or several days, depending on your needs, and your desire to connect to an angel. If you are not sure what you will say when you make contact, spend some more time preparing. You don't need to rehearse everything in a word-perfect way, but you should know why you are making contact. If you are too vague, then the entire experience may feel ambiguous.

The ideal state to attain is one where you are eager, but not desperate, to make contact with the angel, because there is an area of your life that you wish to illuminate or change. You do not need to know all the questions you will ask, but you should have some clarity about the purpose of the contact. If you call on the angel, and the evocation works, it is a terrible waste to say, 'I just wanted to chat about creativity.' But you do not need to be so specific that you say, 'I need help with chapter three of my novel.' Evocation does have a more profound and mystical quality. Although your questions may relate to relatively mundane aspects of yourself and your life, evocation will illuminate them in a way that feels anything but mundane. Know this before you begin, and focus on the needs as you perceive them.

Although this step is absolutely vital, do not be bound by it. If, when you attain contact, you realize there is something else that you actually need to discuss with the angel, then go with that. You can safely assume that the connection has already brought you deeper clarity and uncovered an area of need that is important to you.

Prepare the Space

When you are ready to begin the ritual, find a time to be alone, and ensure that you will not be disturbed. Although you can evoke at any time, and in just about any place, you should spend some time winding down from normal reality before you begin. For at least one hour before you work, stop eating, switch off your phone, and ignore your email. You don't have to become an instant master of mindfulness, but you should become aware of where you are and what you are doing, moment to moment, rather than being lost in thought and distraction. This step is one that many people will attempt to skip, but it is absolutely fundamental to success. Turning down the noise of the world may feel strange, and that's fine. Evocation is not a part of everyday life, and it should not be approached as though it's the next thing you do after watching a YouTube video.

You can sit, kneel or stand, but your primary aim is to be comfortable, without being so relaxed that you're going to sleep. This book, with the angel's sigil, should be near to hand. You may find it more convenient to photocopy or photograph and print the sigil, than to use the book.

You can work at any time of day or night, but you will probably find that certain times appeal to you more than others. Some people love to work before sunrise, and I have to say that this is a time when I find evocation particularly easy. I will go outside, enjoy the cold morning air, settle gently into the day, and then begin the ritual before the sun comes over the horizon. That's great for me, but I know that some people loathe the morning and everything about it, seeing it as a time of struggle, strain and weariness.

If you prefer to work at night, you might be inspired by the twilight that follows sunset, or by working close to midnight. Some people like to work mid-afternoon, or just before lunch, and these times are no less magickal if they appeal to you. Do, however, remain aware of how you feel about the timing. You may plan a specific time, and then feel that it just isn't right. Trust these instincts, and adapt accordingly.

Given that you are trying to create a magickal atmosphere, does it matter where you perform the ritual? Some people really like to go outside, find some special place, or dedicate a room to ritual practice. I can't argue against this, if it works for you, but I prefer to allow any space I am in to become magickal. Although I like working outside, or in large, open rooms that have little in the way of adornment, it is rarely practical to find yourself in such a space. If you're stuck in a small apartment, performing the ritual by your bedside, there is nothing to prevent the magick from working.

If you find that candles, incense and other symbols of magick work for you, then go ahead. I have a very close friend who surrounds herself with a circle of crystals, even though she does not believe they actually do anything. They make it feel more magickal to her, and that is all. I used to use incense, but over time I began to find that it felt more like pollution than anything remotely spiritual. I have used fresh flowers, and find they capture the mood more effectively for me. These days I use nothing.

There are many who believe that incense is an essential ingredient of evocation. I disagree, but if you are tempted by any of these symbolic adornments, then go ahead and use them. If it works for you, that is all that matters. But please do not feel the need to use them. If you are happy to sit on the floor and attempt to contact an angel, with sincere need, and strength of will, that can work. If you are distracted, unprepared and have clouded thoughts, no amount of incense will make an angel appear before you.

Preparing the space can be as simple as closing the door and sitting down, but if you prefer to make a more elaborate ceremony, do whatever works for you. I do not advise the use of drugs or alcohol when performing magick. Other people disagree, but I believe the altered state of conscious is more effective when it arises from your desire to attain contact. An altered state imposed by a substance can actually cloak an evocation, and can potentially make you too far gone to speak with genuine clarity should the evocation be successful.

Some people find it difficult to find places that are truly private, and although I understand that this can be a challenge, do make sure that you won't be disturbed. Being pulled out of an evocation is not in any way dangerous, but can be disorienting and unpleasant, like having ice water thrown in your face. The more secure you are, knowing that you will not be disturbed, the easier you will find it to work the magick.

Build Affinity

This is the core process whereby you encourage an evocation. The technique consists of you reaching for the angel, with your mind, heart and spirit. This is achieved by virtue of the angel's name, the sigil and the Evocation keys you have been given. So for Iophiel you would begin by scanning the sigil in the usual way; that is, scanning your eyes over the words on the outside of the black circle, three times. You would then speak the divine words, ending with Iophiel (pronounced as EE-OH-FEE-ELL).

This part of the process should be familiar, but you turn

up the energy by *willing* a contact between yourself and the angel. You are not simply calling to the angel, but actually trying to forge a connection. You may close your eyes once you have scanned the letters in the sigil, if you find this helps. Remember that will is not the same as force. There should be no strain, only calm determination. Some people imagine that they are reaching to a consciousness hidden behind a massive stone wall. Others imagine they are reaching to a consciousness that is many miles away. You may find these techniques useful for helping to establish the sensation of reaching, but I find it is also useful to imagine that the angel is *already with you*. Assume that Iophiel is here, present, and that there is no resistance, no need to strain. All you are doing is loosening the restrictions of normality, to enable the angel to touch your perceptions. In other words, you reach for the angel's consciousness, and assume it is there. Then you allow your awareness of that reality to grow.

You do not need to keep the sigil in view at all times, but you may find it helps to glance at the sigil from time to time, as you continue to speak the angel's name. This may be slow and soft, or more like a chant. Be guided by your intuition, and what feels right to you.

As you repeat the angel's name, contemplate the angel's Evocation Keys. Doing so helps you to connect with the angel. If you were told to find a small child in a crowd, it would be much easier if you were told that the child was a small, brown-haired girl, wearing a blue hat. These details would give guidance to your search. The Evocation Keys are akin to that. By contemplating them, you reach for the angel more effectively.

You contemplate the Evocation Keys with your imagination. If there is a scent, you imagine the scent. If there is color or other detail, you picture that color or detail. If you have a strong visual imagination, you may prefer to start with the visuals. Others find it easier to imagine the conceptual aspects of the keys, such as the feelings that accompany the angel. For some, scent or sound is easier to imagine. Start with something that is easy for you.

In this example we'll imagine that you find it easy to imagine scents, and so you imagine the scent of floral blossom. You only need a memory of blossom to be able to recreate the scent in your imagination. As you do, continue to say the angel's name, out loud. You may then picture blossom falling. You might see this only in your mind, or if you have a strong imagination, you may picture the blossom falling through the room around you. Allow yourself to see pale blue sky, and a flash of sapphire as you glimpse the robes of Iophiel. As you reach for the presence of Iophiel, notice the strong feelings of love, and also sense the angel's deep courage. This is how you use the Evocation Keys. Simply imagine the keys, while saying the angel's name, and willing a connection to the angel.

You will notice that I don't suggest actually picturing the angel, and this is because any image you impose may be inaccurate. That is not to say that the angel has an objective appearance that is shared by many people. But, if you ever see the angel, the image that arises occurs due to what is offered by the angel, combined with the way that you filter that image with your perception. As such, what you see may not be what you are expecting.

You may see a beautiful, robed angel, with white wings. You may see light. You may see something else altogether, which is beyond the realms of ordinary description. Whatever you see will be right for you, but it is important to let this arise, rather than to deliberately picture it.

This means that rather than picturing the angel, you only imagine aspects of the Evocation Keys. Finding this balance of imagination can be quite tricky, so I suggest that you focus only on imagining the Evocation Keys. Then, if anything else occurs in your imagination, you can assume that is the angel making itself known.

You will notice that some angels are described as having

grace, beauty or other qualities, so what are you supposed to imagine if you don't actually picture the angel? Try to imagine these concepts directly. Imagine what grace feels like. Imagine how it feels to perceive beauty. You may find this easy, or it may take time to get it right. Making the effort is as important as getting it right.

Call to the Angel

Spend some time building your affinity to the angel. You may feel a sense of psychic pressure building up as you do this, or you may simply feel that the time is right to call the angel directly. You have been saying the angel's name, but now you call for the angel to appear.

Say , 'Iophiel, I ask that you appear before me. Iophiel, I ask that you make yourself known to me. Iophiel, I ask for your wisdom.'

You will note that this phrase calls for Iophiel to appear visibly. It then suggests that Iophiel become known to you, which is effectively a request for greater connection, and for you to sense the angel's presence. Finally, you call for the angel's wisdom, and this is a way of saying that you seek connection for the sake of communication.

The wording I suggest here can produce a successful evocation. The wording has been refined over a great deal of time, by many practicing occultists, so use it unless you feel a very strong instinct to use your own words. If you feel an urge to speak your own words, be polite and firm. Do not beg or plead for the angel to appear, but do make sure you name the angel directly.

You have made your request, and the angel will become known to you.

Experience Evocation

Having made the call, evocation will now occur, and you only have to leave a focused time and space for the angel to respond. You do not want to wait, impatiently, but nor do you want to let your mind drift. Losing interest at this point will break the evocation, so keep your focus on the evocation.

The technique I recommend is to keep your eyes open, but unfocussed, so that you are looking into the empty space before you. While resting your gaze on this nothingness, ignoring the mundane reality that may be in your field of vision (you wall, window or whatever else is there), you allow yourself to remain aware of the Evocation Keys. Without staring, let yourself imagine the evocation keys. At the same time, you remain open to the angel's presence. You are no longer reaching, and you are certainly not waiting, but you attain a state that is similar to listening. To illustrate this, imagine you are at an orchestral concert, and the musicians have tuned their instruments, everything is ready to go, and there is the pause of silence before the first notes are struck. You do not wait or hope for the music to start, because you trust that it will. But you listen. You are open to the sound that you know will come. In evocation, you should attempt to enter a similar state, but psychically. You remain open to the angel, allowing it to appear.

This instruction may sound horribly vague, but I can assure you that it is very important that my instructions not be too prescriptive. What I have suggested here is enough, and as you experiment, you will find a way of working that is most effective for you.

At all times, perform evocation with the full expectation that it will work, but without any need for a result. It is possible to be determined, without feeling needy, and this is the state you should achieve.

If nothing happens, and a few minutes, or half an hour has passed, do you declare the evocation a failure? You do not. Although we talk about 'successful' evocation, every evocation is successful, because you have grown closer to the angel you are attempting to contact. If nothing obvious happens it only means that you need to practice, and that you need to refine these techniques. Patience, persistence, courage. It can be very difficult to continue with this magick if it doesn't work the way you want it to, but one of the most important techniques is to reject the emotion of discouragement. You do the work, you evoke, and you allow evocation to be what it will be.

The experience of a successful evocation may be extremely clear, even quite dramatic, or it may be a subtle nudging at your consciousness. My own experiences are so varied that I could fill a book describing them. I have heard descriptions from many people, and evocation is so variable, and at times so difficult to describe, that nothing I write here can genuinely prepare you. Sometimes, you feel a connection to another consciousness, and it feels so ordinary, that only later do you realise that anything happened. Sometimes you see the angel, standing before you, filling the room with light and devastating you with awe. Sometimes, you have thoughts that don't quite feel like your own, and on reflection you realise these were angelic contact. Sometimes you hear spoken words. Whatever the level of apparent reality of your evocation, any time there is a connection, it is a successful evocation.

The experience will be your own. The aim of evocation, of course, is to commune with the angel. You may achieve this immediately. You may find that the angel listens, gives answers, and communicates with you regarding your desires. You may charge the angel with a task, and be given a sense of how the magick is going to work. You may experience this only as a slight sense of awareness, so slight that you're not sure whether or not you're fooling yourself. You may see light, you may see sparkles, you may see darkness, blurring of light, detect scents, feel a presence, feel warmth or cold, or the tingling of a strange atmosphere as the supernatural opens up in your world.

If the evocation is successful, one thing you will probably notice is a moment where your reality seems to click, switch over or change substantially. The sense of altered reality goes from being hazy and distant, to being quite concrete. This mental 'click' can happen even with a vague evocation, where you only sense the angel's presence; something just seems to click, and you know evocation has been achieved. It can also happen when the angel is visible. Even after the angel has appeared, there is often a moment where something seems to click into place more completely, both mentally and psychically, and you know that contact has been fully established, and it's time to communicate.

You will notice that when I write about this subject, it is not as clear, straightforward or even as easy to follow as most magickal instruction. That is quite deliberate, and this is how I have been guided to write this chapter. I should not describe the experience too accurately or restrictively. Be open to whatever happens.

When evoking spirits, most occultists will tell you that it is usually wise to test and question the spirit, to make sure it is the spirit that you have called, and not an imposter. In theory, it is possible for another spirit to take the place of the spirit you have called. In practice, this is not as common as many people suggest, but testing spirits is a sensible precaution. However, the Affinity Process itself is a better filter, and a better predictor of authentic contact, than any form of questioning or testing. As such, I believe that the experience you obtain when following these instructions is safe and authentic, and you have nothing to fear.

Close the Space

At some point, the evocation will end. This may because you feel there is nothing more to be achieved, or the contact is too vague, or it may be because the angel suggests that the evocation is over. Many times, the angel simply withdraws without warning. This can produce a moment of shock that feels almost like grief, but do not be alarmed by this sensation. It is usually replaced with elation as you emerge from the evocation.

To close the space, remove the sigil from sight (by closing the book, for example), and bring your focus back to where you are.

There are many methods for returning to normality, and they do not need to be ritualistic. You can just slap your face, come back to normality, look out the window, and that is enough. My preferred method is to clap my hands, loudly and sharply, hard enough for it to feel almost painful. I clap three times. I then speak my name, as I stand up.

It's a good idea to leave the room, eat something, go out and do something else. You may have an urge to write about the experience. If so, do write it all down, but do this in another room, so that you aren't drawn back into the trance-like feelings of evocation.

There is no need to banish. Simply choosing to come back to normal reality is enough to end the magick. It's akin to waking up. When you're waking up, the sensation of dream sometimes lingers, but rarely for long, because the real world does not feel like a dream. After an evocation, you may experience the world as exceptionally mundane, while also sensing the magickal reality that underlies everything; this contradictory perception is quite common, and can feel strange at first, but everyday normality is usually restored within minutes or hours.

Evocation is not always easy, and the mental balancing act required for it to be successful can take time to acquire. Be aware, though, that some people experience a full evocation on the first attempt, and this can be almost overwhelming. As such, it is strongly recommended that you only go ahead with this magick if you are absolutely of sound mind. A friend of mine says that nobody of sound mind performs evocation, but his tongue is firmly in his cheek. The experience can be quite intense, so do look after yourself, and if at any point it feels like it's too much, rest for a while and come back to this magick at another time.

When you experience evocation, your life is never the same again, so I hope that these instructions help you to access this glorious connection to the angels.

The Evocation Keys

The Evocation Keys for Orpaniel, Boel, Gavriel, Iophiel, Tumiel, and Tzadkiel

Orpaniel appears as an angel of great beauty, standing before a stormy ocean. Around the angel there is a brilliant blue-white glow. There is the scent of cedar and the feeling of the wind on your skin. Orpaniel yields a sensation of grace and majesty.

Boel appears as a beautiful angel, bathed in white light, tinged with violet. Boel conveys a sense of love and compassion. There is the sense of clean, still air.

Gavriel appears in robes of brilliant white. The angel conveys a sense of kindness and joy. There is the impression of gently moving air.

Iophiel appears in sapphire blue robes, against a pale blue sky. White blossom falls through the air. There is the floral scent of blossom. The angel conveys a feeling of love and courage.

Tumiel appears robed in silver and blue. Clean, fresh air rushes through, scented with cedar. There is a strong atmosphere of kindness and serenity.

Tzadkiel is robed in violet and blue, emanating brilliant white light. The angel conveys a sense of grace and balance.

The Evocation Keys for Kavtziel, Ravchiel, Oziel, Shemshiel, Tofiel and Nagriel

Kavtziel is robed in crimson, with an aura of white and gold flames. The angel conveys kind strength, and there is the scent of warm metal.

Ravchiel appears robed in scarlet and orange, conveying a sense of warmth and certainty. There is a scent like burning leaves.

Oziel wears robes of gold and white, and has an aura of hazy, orange flame. The angel brings a feeling of certainty, and the scent of rocks heated by the sun.

Shemshiel is robed in scarlet. The angel appears shimmering against a black, starless sky, and conveys a sense of immense strength.

Tofiel is an angel of might and kindness, who appears robed in white, with an aura of white light. There is a scent of charcoal.

Nagriel is robed in scarlet and black, emanating a golden light and the feeling of strength. There is a scent of scorched paper.

The Evocation Keys for Nachliel, Gavoriel, Dahniel, Yehodiel, Kevashiel and Shahariel

Nachliel appears as an angel of beauty, standing before a still lake at sunset (so still that it appears as a golden mirror). The angel conveys a sense of calm.

Gavoriel is robed in gold and amber, and feels noble and compassionate. This beautiful angel also conveys a sense of harmony.

Dahniel wears robes of gold, and emanates a strong light, as from the midday sun. There is scent like fresh rosemary.

Yehodiel is robed in amber, bathed in the pink light of sunset. There is the scent of garden flowers, and warmth like the end of a still, summery afternoon.

Kevashiel appears as a beautiful angel, in robes the color of a pale pink rose, bathed in light the color of honey. There is the scent of rain on grass.

Shahariel is an angel of beauty and grace, robed in gold. The angel conveys a sense of compassion, and is accompanied by a sharp spicy scent, like freshly cut ginger.

The Evocation Keys for
Berachiel, Tahftiel, Rachmiel, Tzafuniel, Trumiel and Gedodiel

Berachiel wears glowing emerald robes and stands before a cloudless sky at twilight. The angel conveys sensual love, and is accompanied by the scent of a fresh rose.

Tahftiel stands before a starry sky, robed in emerald, and warmed by a coppery light. The angel brings a sense of confidence.

Rachmiel is robed in yellow and red, like autumn leaves. An angel of beauty, Rachmiel brings a strong sense of communal love, and the scent of warm metal.

Tzafuniel appears as a beautiful angel, robed in forest green, but emanating a coppery light. There is the scent of sandalwood.

Trumiel is robed in copper and gold. This beautiful angel appears in the shimmer of a heat haze, and is accompanied by the sound of wind in leaves.

Gedodiel is an angel of intense beauty, robed in amber, standing before a lush green forest. The angel brings a strong feeling of love, and the scent of fresh earth.

The Evocation Keys for Cheziel, Kumiel, Barkiel, Tahariel, Nuriel and Amiel

Cheziel appears as an angel of beauty, robed in dark red robes. The angel conveys an atmosphere of truth.

Kumiel is robed in white, on a landscape of flat stone, bathed in amber light. There is the scent of lime and a sense of a bright, alert intellect.

Barkiel appears as an angel of yellowish white, like a misty winter sunrise. There is the sound of humming. The angel conveys a sense of living energy.

Tahariel is robed in russet red, and bathed in an orange glow like sunset. The angel brings the scent of lavender, and conveys a feeling of great honour.

Nuriel is a beautiful angel, who appears robed in amber (the color of sunlight passing through honey). There is the scent of lemon and the feeling of sunshine on skin.

Amiel is an angel of great beauty and understanding, who appears robed in dark amber.

The Evocation Keys for
Yisrael, Gahdiel, Lahaviel,
Pahniel, Zachriel and Kedoshiel

Yisrael appears as a strong angel, dressed in robes of such dark blue they are almost black. The angel stands in a fallow field lit by moonlight, accompanied by the scent of cut grass.

Gahdiel is an angel robed in white, bright as a full moon, standing before a dark, starry sky. The angel conveys great strength.

Lahaviel appears as a white angel, surrounded by a violet glow. There is the scent of blossom, and a sense of intense stillness.

Pahniel is seen as a moon-white angel, against a dark blue background, like the sky at late twilight.

Zachriel appears as a powerful angel, robed in ivory, against a dark, indigo sky. There is a sweet, floral scent.

Kedoshiel appears as an angel of silvery light, standing before a moonlit river. You sense cold night air, and the scent of wet stone.

The Evocation Keys for Shelgiel, Karviel, Vaviel Tzuriel, Ialpiel and Tavriel

Shelgiel appears as an angel of justice and power, wearing robes of black and gold. The scents of ivy and earth are present.

Karviel is robed in gold (like sunset light), and has an aura of pale blue. The angel conveys kind certainty. There is an air of clean salt water.

Vaviel appears in dark red robes, but the air around the angel is like a light blue mist. This is an atmosphere of strength and justice, and the scent of pine.

Tzuriel conveys an atmosphere of spiritual power. The angel appears bathed in blue and golden light. White blossom falls around the angel, and you smell the rich scent of fertile earth.

Ialpiel appears as an angel of great calm and power, standing in a field of ripe wheat. A bluish glow emanates from the angel, and you smell the rich scent of the wheat. When Ialpiel is present, you sense a strong atmosphere of mystery.

Tavriel is seen robed in black, surrounded by an aura of blue flame. You smell unburnt coal. Tavriel brings the sense of distance or journey, and places that you have not yet been.

The Hidden Power of Evocation

Earlier in the book I told you that this magick is largely aimed at yourself, but a hidden power of evocation is the ability to direct the magick so that it affects others. When you evoke successfully, you have the ability to direct the result to another person. This can be used to gift a positive quality to somebody you care about, or indeed to influence and compel the individual to act in accordance with your will. If you are uncomfortable using influence magick then pay this no heed, but if this style of magick appeals, know that it is an option.

To illustrate this, look at the second Angel in this book, Boel, who works with truth. When you need to hear the truth from another, Boel can compel the other person to speak to you more truthfully. If ever you suspect that somebody is holding back the truth, work with this angel to compel the other party to open up to you. Whether you feel a great secret is being hidden, or just require more open communication, Boel can open the way. To do so, you evoke Boel, and tell the angel the result that you want. You may receive the answer immediately, from the angel, or the person in question may speak to you more openly in the coming days.

For every angel in this book, the powers can be adapted to work on others. Once you have an understanding of the angel's powers, and the areas that it can affect, it is easy to work out how it can be used to influence others. Gavriel could bestow strength on somebody you care about. Tumiel can encourage somebody with a closed heart to feel unconditional love. Shahariel could cause another person to appreciate their love for you. Oziel could help a loved one to overcome a bad habit, without them ever knowing that you called on the angel. Indeed, this work of influence, whether performed with altruistic intentions or not, should be performed in absolute secrecy. Even when the result has come to pass, do not let the recipient know that the magick ever took place.

If you are able to evoke the angel, you can speak your request. Do so firmly and clearly, without begging or explaining why you want the result, unless the angel asks you directly. Simply state what you want to happen, and how you want the other person to be influenced.

Evocation is far from predictable, so there are no guarantees that this form of influence magick will always work in the way that you imagine. Sometimes, the angel will give you a vision, or impression of another truth that sheds light on your desire, rather than fulfilling your desire in the expected way. This is not the angel defying you, so much as the angel responding with a higher truth. Be warned that this can be alarming, but also enlightening.

The Source of Angelic Knowledge

There are many divine names used to call these angels. You may feel a strong urge to know exactly what you are saying during a ritual. When calling on the first six angels in this book, for example, you say Zadkiel, Abagitatz, Adirirotz, Bahirirotz, Guhviryaron, Yigbahyah, Tlamyah, Tztania, followed by the angel's name. What does all this mean?

The first word is the name of the archangel overseeing the operation; in this case, Zadkiel. The second word is comprised of six letters taken from The Forty-Two Letter Name of God; in this case, it's Abagitatz. Following that, you read a set of six divine names.

It's important to know that these divine words and names do not succumb to direct translation in the ordinary way. Simply typing the names into an online translator will not yield anything of use. Even if you type in the Hebrew (as seen in the outer ring of the sigil), you won't find what you're looking for, and that is because there is a long and complicated history behind the names.

For example, Adirirtotz, which is a variation of Adiriron, is a name that speaks of a mighty singing voice. Although this name yields to translation, to some extent, many of the names do not, because they are, after all, divine names. *They are abstractions of thought and divine power, rather than ordinary words.* They are letter combinations that reach for the divine, and should be thought of as an encoding of divine power, rather than words in the mundane sense.

I am often asked to provide an English translation of such names, but as there is none, all I can do here is provide a reasonable English transliteration of the names.

The first six angels are Orpaniel, Boel, Gavriel, Iophiel, Tumiel and Tzadkiel, and they are associated with the archangel Zadkiel, the letter group Abagitatz, and divine names Adirirotz, Bahirirotz, Guhviryaron, Yigbahyah,

Tlamyah and Tztania. (You may notice that the archangel overseeing the operation is called Zadkiel, and that one of the angels is called Tzadkiel, and that in Hebrew and in the sigils, the spelling of these names is identical. So are these the same angels? This is an academic point, but for the sake of your work you can think of them as different aspects of the same power. The archangel Zadkiel overseas the powers of the first six angels listed here, but Tzadkiel is called as a specific and distinct angel. As with all theory, this is open to endless debate and speculation, but in practical terms it is useful to know that there is an archangel called Zadkiel, and that when you call the angel Tzadkiel, the angel has a distinct presence and atmosphere.)

The next six angels are Kavtziel, Ravchiel, Oziel, Shemshiel, Tofiel and Nagriel and they are associated with the archangel Camael, the letter group Karastan and the divine names Kudamyah, Rugaryah, Riryah, Shuhgayah, Tuhlatyah, and Nuhariyah.

The next six angels are Nachliel, Gavoriel, Dahniel, Yehodiel, Kevashiel and Shahariel and they are associated with the archangel Raphael, the letter group Nagdikesh and the divine names Nishmaryah, Guharyah, Duharyah, Yuhalyah, Kasiyah and Shigyonyah. (The archangel Raphael is well known in Western culture, although it is usually pronounced as something like RAFF-EYE-ELL. Here, we use the pronunciation RAH-FAH-ELL. As always, correct pronunciation is not essential, but this is pointed out so that you know the word RAH-FAH-ELL calls on the archangel Raphael.)

The next six angels are Berachiel, Tahftiel, Rachmiel, Tzafuniel, Trumiel and Gedodiel and they are associated with the archangel Haniel, the letter group Batartztag, and the divine names Boalyah, Todaryah, Ramyah, Tzatztsiyah, Tahavhiyah and Galgalyah.

The next six angels are Cheziel, Kumiel, Barkiel, Tahariel, Nuriel and Amiel and they are associated with the archangel Michael, the letter group Chakabetna and the divine names Chinanayah, Katakayah, Buhavuhavuya, Tavhoyah, Nuhtanyah and Amamayah. (The archangel Michael is well known in Western culture, but is usually pronounced like the English boy's name Michael, which is something like MIKE-ULL. Here, we use the pronunciation ME-CHAH-ELL. Exact pronunciation is not essential, but this is pointed out so that you know the word ME-CHAH-ELL calls on the archangel Michael.)

The next six angels are Yisrael, Gahdiel, Lahaviel, Pahniel, Zachriel and Kedoshiel and they are associated with the archangel Gabriel, the letter group Yagalpzok and the divine names Yuhalshurayah, Gawdirayah, Luhmimaryah, Puhkorkaryah, Zahrayah and Kuhmalyah. (The archangel Gabriel is well known in Western culture, but is usually pronounced something like GAY-BREE-ELL. Here, we use the pronunciation GAH-BREE-ELL, which is only a slight variation.)

The final six angels are Shelgiel, Karviel, Vaviel, Tzuriel, Ialpiel and Tavriel and they are associated with the archangel Sandalphon, the letter group Shakavtzyat and the divine names Shathodrayah, Kadoshyah, Vuhahaleilyah, Tzadyah, Yithadriyah and Tamteilyah.

When you look at your chosen sigil, the above words and names appear in the outer circle, starting at the top, with the archangel name, going anti-clockwise (because Hebrew is read from right to left). The angel's name appears in the centre of the sigil, again written from right to left. It is this combination of Hebrew letters that gives you access to angelic power.

You may also wonder if the angels named here are the same as angels mentioned in other books. Dahniel, for example, is listed here as an angel who can restore balance, but in *The 72 Angels of Magick*, Daniel (spelt identically in Hebrew, and pronounced exactly the same way) is an angel who assists with decisions and communication. So are these

165

the same angels?

My personal experience of these angels has led me to believe that the *manner* of the calling affects exactly *what* you are calling. So when you call using the method in this book, you access a different power to that found when using the method found in other books. This remains true even if the angels can objectively be said to be the same.

When I have conversed with the Dahniel mentioned in this book, using this book's methods, I get an impression that is quite unlike the impression I get from the Daniel mentioned in *The 72 Angels of Magick*.

Sometimes, however, there are correspondences. I have, for example, called on the Daniel in *The 72 Angels of Magick*, and have noted the scent of fresh rosemary, which is associated with the Dahniel in this book.

To me, the answer is not clear cut, and even with decades of magickal experience I do not have a simple answer to this question. Even when the angels have been questioned on this matter, during direct evocation, they have given obscure or hazy answers, as they often do when questioned about the nature of their reality. Your own experience may give you more insight.

For the sake of practical magick, however, a good starting point is to work with the powers as listed in each book, rather than assuming that similarly named angels are necessarily one and the same.

If you're wondering where we found out about these angels, you should know that most of the angels listed here do not appear in the standard angel dictionaries and New Age texts of modern publishing, because they belong to a more hidden tradition of magick. If you want to do your own research, you will find reference to these angels in texts such as *Oedipus Aegyptiacus* (although it's written in Latin), or *Shorshei ha-Shemot* (but that's written in Hebrew).

I point this out to show that these angels are not mere constructs of modern magick, but have been referenced consistently in magickal texts for many ages. Although you are free to do your own research, the purpose of this book is to show how centuries of knowledge, and decades of practical magick, can be blended into a direct magickal method.

It is not my purpose to explore the theory of what the angels are, or to proclaim which ancient text has the most accurate descriptions, correspondences and sigils. My own connection to these angels did not come from primary sources, but from a private grimoire – an extensive collection of occult material that shows how the older methods have been adapted and streamlined. This work has been further refined by The Gallery of Magick into the methods that you find in this book. While based in tradition, it has been modernized and simplified.

The names and powers of the angels vary across the texts from which they are drawn. The only way to make sense of this is through experience. Everything you find in this book has been refined in accordance with the experience of direct contact and communication with the angels. I believe that the accumulated experience of many occultists is more important than any single source. Equally, your own experience may be unique. When working with an angel, you may gain insights into aspects of that angel that are unknown to us. Should you develop such a personal connection, treasure it.

Please note that the information in this chapter is provided only for those who are curious. I occasionally receive messages from people saying, 'I don't know what I'm saying, so how do I know I'm not calling on the devil?' Although it is my firm belief that people who fear magick should steer clear of magick, I also appreciate that a little clarification is sometimes required. So what I provide above is only a small indication of what is being said, along with the nature of the angels, but should you wish to research further, this may be a helpful starting point. I should add, however, that no amount of armchair research will ever get you a magickal result. Perform some magick, and then you will *experience* magick.

Working with Magick

The magick in this book works easily for most people, but if you find it difficult, *The Gallery of Magick* website blog contains many FAQs, along with advice and practical information that is updated on a regular basis.

www.galleryofmagick.com

The Gallery of Magick Facebook page will also keep you up to date.

If you have an interest in developing your magick further, there are many texts that can assist you.

A companion text to this book is *The 72 Sigils of Power* by Zanna Blaise. Zanna was a major contributor to the methods employed in *The Angels of Alchemy*. In *The 72 Sigils of Power*, she covers Contemplation Magic (for insight and wisdom) and Results Magic (for changing the world around you). She is also the author of *The Angels of Love*, which uses the tasking method with six angels from this book, to heal relationships and to attract a soulmate.

Words of Power and *The Greater Words of Power* present an extremely simple ritual practice, for bringing about change in yourself and others, as well as directing and attracting changed circumstances.

For those seeking more money, *Magickal Cashbook* uses a ritual to attract small bursts of money out of the blue, and works best when you are not desperate, but when you can approach the magick with a sense of enjoyment and pleasure. *Magickal Riches* is more comprehensive, with rituals for everything from gambling to sales, with a master ritual to oversee magickal income. For the more ambitious, *Wealth Magick* contains a complex set of rituals for earning money by building a career. For those still trying to find their feet, there is *The Magickal Job Seeker*.

Magickal Protection contains rituals that can be directed at specific problems, as well as a daily practice called The Sword Banishing, which is one of our most popular and effective rituals. For those who cannot find peace through protection there is *Magickal Attack*, by Gordon Winterfield. Dark magick is not to everybody's taste, but this is a highly moral approach that puts the emphasis on using authority to restore peace.

Magickal Seduction is a text that looks at attracting others by using magick to amplify your attractive qualities, rather than through deception. *Adventures in Sex Magick* is a more specialized text, for those open minded enough to explore this somewhat extreme form of magick.

The Master Works of Chaos Magick by Adam Blackthorne is an overview of self-directed and creative magick, which also includes a section covering the Olympic Spirits. *Magickal Servitors* takes another aspect of Chaos Magick and updates it into a modern, workable method.

The 72 Angels of Magick is our most comprehensive book of angel magick, and explores hundreds of powers that can be applied by working with these angels.

Damon Brand

www.galleryofmagick.com

Printed in Poland
by Amazon Fulfillment
Poland Sp. z o.o., Wrocław